Paren
Children with
ADHD

Therapy Strategies for Managing Kids Behavior, Improving Attention, Cultivating Calmness, and Reducing Anxiety with Mindfulness and Acceptance

Sarah Snowden

LEGAL DISCLAIMER

Contents

INTRODUCTION

This book is meant for parents of children dealing with attention deficit / hyperactivity disorder (ADHD), whether or not they already receive treatment for their children. It will encourage you in a better way to understand ADHD and bring you with your child on a different course. You will discover new ways to prevent the development of ADHD behavior and help your child meet expectations more effectively on his own and through communicating with others. You'll know that ADHD isn't a lifelong disorder. ADHD is something your kid is doing rather than something he has. It's a personality trait, not a medical condition.

Have you found that when participating in an event he initiates and loves, your child is much less hyperactive, impulsive and inattentive? For starters, he might be able to play for hours on end with interlocking blocks if left to himself. Time for self-directed play is very important for kids, and they may not like to have to adapt to the limits of their behavior and other activities they do. Kids may feel uncomfortable being guided or forced to act in some respects, and this anxiety makes ADHD behavior more likely. Sadly, kids need to have limitations and expectations because they have not yet understood about life's risks and needs.

So how do you describe forms that are easy for both of you to interact? How do you get your kid to agree when he tries to do something else without any trouble? How can you help him assume responsibility and autonomy slowly as he needs you to do something for him? How can you get him to follow when nobody watches over him?

You'll see when you read this book that it's not all that rough. But be willing to be patient. While threats and demands can produce instant conformity, it is vastly superior to help your child learn self-reliance and cooperation, but it can take much longer. Occasionally, if your actions are effective, you may be uncertain. For instance, if your child throws a tantrum and you don't react, in the short term, you essentially allow the unwelcomed behavior. But in the long term, your unwillingness to feed into the drama can be very successful. You may also worry if you're lenient or if you're letting your kid get away with wrongdoing when you're using this new parenting style.

You might think you're incompetent or you're not doing everything you can to get out of his issues. The techniques in this book, though, are not at all permissive. You can find that as you bring them into use, you are more assertive and strong than you were. And the sooner you start, the earlier.

The book will help make the child's behavior more mature. Finally, instead of relying on your notes, he will do more on his own. You should pay more attention to the needs of others and behave in ways that make life easier for both of you.

You must take one or more of the following four acts as you bring this new parenting style into effect. These behaviors of parenting constitute the basis of the method, so keep them in mind. They are your basic tools, and throughout this book, you will learn how to use them.

Chapter 1
So Your Child Has an ADHD Diagnosis

Your child did not come with a manual. Parenting can be a hard job to start with, and you are now facing the difficult task of managing an ADHD-diagnosed child. You may receive advice from many people, laypersons and professionals alike, and you may hear many different ideas about what's wrong with your child. Who do you think? What's the best thing to do?

THE USUAL BEGINNING

The scenario most often goes like this: a child of school age is constantly noisy in the classroom and does not follow instructions. The teacher suggests that the child be assessed for ADHD to the parents. The parents are not surprised— they are worrying because at home, the child was also hard to handle. Often the child seems to be "driven by a motor" and "out of control."

The child might shriek and be hard to soothe. Perhaps the child had a medical or developmental disability that made it difficult for her to meet expectations. Perhaps when she was a child, she was very busy and seemed to have a short span of concentration, picking up toys just to lose interest in them quickly. The family may have thought for years that something was wrong, and now others say it's ADHD.

It's fascinating that this diagnosis is obtained by so many of our kids (especially boys). According to a US study from 2009, most often, an alarming 9% of our children aged four to seventeen receive an ADHD diagnosis from the Department of Health and Human Services. Is it because, instead of socializing, these kids spend too much time in front of the Television and computer screens? For example, are boys more involved and more difficult to manage at home and at school? In our homes, isn't there enough discipline? Are we too worried to make our kids happy and not show them the boundaries? Are we too busy to be effective? Are we so concerned about security that we are hindering many of our children from achieving self-direction and independence? Or are we simply improving the identification of children with disabilities due to improvements in our health care system?

The Presumption of Impairment

Many people believe that ADHD is a lasting developmental disability that will affect an individual throughout their lives. Some people speculate that, before they act, those with ADHD are less able to stop, look, listen and think. The specific criteria for ADHD can be found in the Mental Disorders Diagnostic and Statistical Manual (DSM) (American Psychiatric Association, 2000). The guide outlines the hyperactive, impulsive and inattentive habits that children may display in order to receive the tag of ADHD.

Children may exhibit the habits described in the DSM for many different reasons. Yet speaking about ADHD as a developmental delay caused by genes, like height or colorblindness, is now very popular. It leads us to believe that the sick will have to accept their fate. We have to deal with the stigma of having an inferior body to others. Their delay will lead them to make careless mistakes, and they will find it harder to prepare, schedule, and pay attention. We will be less able to complete assignments, follow directions, handle duties on a daily basis, and recall what they should do.

To children with ADHD, most clinicians are now prescribing therapy and strict discipline. Because it is unlikely that children with ADHD will be aware of the long-term benefits of cooperation, it is believed that adults in their world must provide them with immediate rewards and punishments to coax them to meet expectations. Throughout the day, they must supervise and remind the children to comply with social standards, one step at a time. However, there is no cure in this view: children with ADHD will never be able, like others, to "put on the brakes."

Starting Treatment

The method for the treatment of ADHD and prescribed treatments can be overwhelming and frustrating. If your child has been diagnosed with ADHD, if she is more independent, you might like it, but that may now seem like an impossible dream. However, once you begin the prescribed therapies, you'll probably notice that the narcotics and strict discipline improve their focus very rapidly and help their skyrocket efficiency.

If your child receives accommodation in school, you may also see immediate improvements. Organizational supports prompt, extended time to complete assignments, new books, and increased incentives and penalties would possibly spark appropriate habits. You may wish you had started the recommended treatments even earlier when she finishes her assignments and shows good behavior.

The Downside of Looking at ADHD in This Way

Although if you follow the usual guidelines, there seem to be significant and meaningful results, the methods will not help your child learn self-reliance and collaboration. So you're not going to find out if she will. You may even produce unwanted side effects that you are unaware of when you act as a warden who puts pressure on your daughter to cooperate by doling out or removing services that are valuable to her.

With this treatment, a child may start learning a variety of ways to counteract attempts to govern her or come to rely even more on her parents to make sure she is doing what she is supposed to do. Instead of worrying about her mother-father relationship, she can begin to focus more on the benefits they command. Without an expected payment, she may not learn about the joy of working together, and that will affect her relationships throughout her life.

There is also another concern: how do children with ADHD learn to control themselves? Strictness and control pressure them to obey, but such discipline does not allow them to develop autonomy. And if nobody makes these kids learn to behave acceptably without treatment, coercion, and scrutiny, how can we ever expect them to? Because as they grow older, they will be harder to monitor, this concern will increase as children approach adolescence.

Potential Drawbacks of Medication

The decision to medicate your child is between you and your child's doctor. You may choose to use medications alone, or you may find it appropriate to use them in combination with other forms of therapy. It is very likely the medicine will quiet the kid down and make her concentrate and do her work. Medication, however, may have disadvantages that are not always immediately evident.

You will be told by prescribers that ADHD medications are effective and benign, but how much of any drug is completely safe? Side effects may escalate over time, and it may become difficult to reverse biological and psychological changes as long as a drug persists in the body. There are rumors that ADHD medications can take a toll on the brain, and there are still unexplained long-term effects on very young children.

Medicinal therapy can also eliminate the problem's severity. Urgency is what drives people to work hard and change, and lack of urgency can diminish your child's desire to seek counseling. You can end up relying entirely on the drugs. But what if the drugs stop working?

Postponing psychotherapy will make things much harder. As kids are older, modifying their patterns and behaviors is not as easy for them. The phrase comes to mind, "You can't teach new tricks to an old dog." Having your kid on long-term medications can also mean higher doses of more drugs as time goes on. Your daughter may need more drugs as she grows up, and her body may also build up immunity for the drug. Unfortunately, with the quantity and number of medications needed to achieve the desired effects, the risk for side effects increases.

Medicinal treatment may also give rise to the assumption that medicine is necessary for success when there may possibly be other ways of solving problems. Individuals can learn to look for psychiatric drugs as a primary way to improve their lives and never investigate whether they can solve their problems differently.

It's also hard to stop medical therapy once it's started (even if monitored by a doctor). Stopping medicine ensures that your daughter must emotionally and physically adapt not to have a chemical reinforcement to her system. Unwanted symptoms can arise as soon when you remove the medicine, and then you're "back to square one." But most notably, while the medical medication is certainly a reasonable treatment option when the advantages greatly outweigh the damage, the long-term benefits for ADHD treatments have not been outstanding. Also, staunch supporters for medicinal therapy admit that when children become adults, medicinal therapy during infancy does not yield better long-term effects.

One example is the major ADHD research by the MTA Cooperative Team. While the initial results revealed that the procedure was the best, subsequent results showed that the effects would not last. Medicated children no longer performed better than children who had undergone other therapies in as little as three years.

ADHD medications are not better therapies, according to William Pelham, a major contributor to the MTA report. Pelham is worried that ADHD medications can adversely affect the height and weight of a boy. He claims that in the treatment of ADHD drugs would play a lesser role.

Decisions

So what does this all mean? You should provide stimulant medication to your child and realize that you will see significant and lasting results most of the time. However, there is a likelihood of short-lived progress. Eventually, relying solely on medications may be ill-advised, although the treatments can take away symptoms fairly quickly and easily.

Nevertheless, there may be times when a medication may be useful for short-term use. Perhaps the concerns of your child are so serious that you need to get quick relief. If she is in a medicated condition, it may be easier to start teaching your child self-reliance and teamwork. And maybe some of the benefits you get from pharmaceutical therapies will persist if you want to through the medications down the road so eventually eliminate them. Just be mindful that there are potential risks and vulnerabilities in medical care.

A New Understanding and Treatment for ADHD

Given the new research which alerts us about using medicine to treat ADHD, it's time to look at ADHD through a different lens and use a completely different approach to the problem — time for what psychologists might consider a "paradigm shift." Without a doubt, you've found moments where your kid becomes concentrated and following instructions without treatment or strict supervision. The diagnosis simply indicates that at the planned moments, she does not do such activities often enough.

A new interpretation of ADHD is provided in this book. You will no longer believe that your child has a medical problem which prevents her from meeting the standards imposed by others, but does not prevent her from pursuing her own interests. You probably already know your child is more talented than anyone else would have you believed. If you could support her with the same passion and commitment, she displays with projects she loves and likes that would change the lion's share of her issues.

For example, most children with ADHD can know that there is some food in the fridge but don't remember to close the kitchen drawer until taking a fork to eat it with. Many are noisy and careless while their parent is on the phone, but as still as a mouse when their bedtime is interrupted by the phone call.

Many will say they don't know how to arrange their house, but many of the same children will organize their figures of action into complex scenes of war. Many will forget homework but don't forget to bring their friends ' trading cards to school. Many will burst out offensive things that turn heads when their parents want them to admit wrongdoing, but don't make a peep. While composing thank-you cards, most wander off track, but when writing Christmas lists, they work feverishly. And many will be lackadaisical about tasks but set the table beautifully when their parents are buttered for a favor.

All of this can lead you to wonder if there can be a biological problem that works in the way ADHD works. If the delays of your child are genetic, their self-management problems would be normal and not so closely associated with specific situations. ADHD is known to be similar to a need for glasses or a hearing aid, but what is the issue of seeing or listening when a person is not involved in it? This comes as no surprise that for years parents have been calling for experts, "Why can my daughter perform so well when she does what she wants to do?" Returning to a psychological perspective on the issue may be a good idea. What if ADHD behavior is something your child has mastered, rather than being related to inborn differences in brain structure or chemistry? Let's presume that this kind of action creates a positive outcome in the life of your son, in certain circumstances.

Psychologists point to this as motivation when the result of an action has a beneficial effect because it enhances or improves the behavior, making it more likely to occur again. Can you identify some of your child's benefits or advantages when she shows behavior with ADHD?

Keep in mind that what might improve your child may not be what you may find appropriate or in the best interests of your child. She can either get anything she loves or get rid of something she doesn't want. You can change the behavior of your child in this way of thinking by changing the way she profits when she shows behavior with ADHD.

Chapter 2

Understanding ADHD Behavior as Reinforced

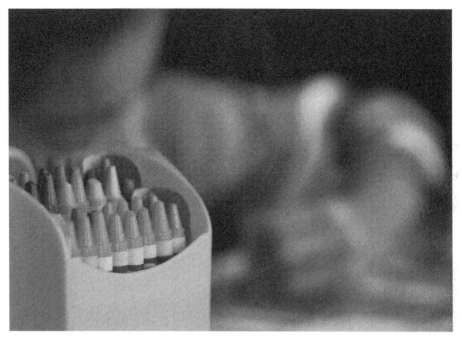

The first thing to realize is that while you and other adults see the ADHD behavior of your child as a problem to overcome, the behavior of ADHD holds solutions for your child to the difficulties he faces on a daily basis. ADHD conduct somehow mitigates the problem when the child faces hardship. By identifying what gives its staying power to its ADHD behavior, you will gain valuable insight into why such behavior so often repeats itself. You'll also take a giant step forward in knowing how to get rid of it.

Training requires repeating what works. When you excel in doing something in a certain way, you'll probably do the same thing again the next time you're in that position. For example, once you figure out that pressing a certain button flips on an appliance, you go straight for that button the next time you want to use the appliance. While you might believe that ADHD behavior could not possibly be changed, just wait and see.

Conformity and Accommodation

ADHD activity is more common in the broadest sense when the child is faced with adversity. Children's hardship can take many different forms. One kind of difficulty for your child is when he has to adhere to the constraints and standards of someone else. ADHD behavior, unless the kid does something he likes, is far less possible. ADHD actions may seem to vanish once the child feels relaxed and happy.

This is why it is unlikely that your son will be hyperactive, impulsive, or inattentive when doing what he needs to do. He will work at his own speed, and enjoy himself, while the child is in control. He doesn't worry about meeting expectations when the activity is his own. He doesn't have to satisfy the needs of anyone else. If he needs to, he will start and stop. His does not feel trapped by other people's expectations and constraints, so less squirming and pain can arise. He only continues when he's comfortable as he takes his own lead; he doesn't have to be vulnerable to unnecessary threats. He has much more control over what happens relative to the roles that others perform and assess.

Children are not required to meet other people's demands, so these issues don't happen early in life. But it is necessary to achieve and adapt to a greater degree for infants and young children. When your child grows older, higher expectations will result in conflicts of interest. Your will may be different from what others want from what your child wants.

Many kids show ADHD tendencies when addressing the problem of who is going to satisfy who. Conflicts arise while waiting, swapping, transitioning, or requiring others to go first. We lag behind in assuming responsibility and are less likely to meet the needs, expectations, and desires of others. We overreact when we lose and when they don't get their way, they become intolerant. Their acts create social as well as academic problems because they do not respond appropriately to what others expect. The behavior is consistent with what we expect from children when they first react to boundaries and limitations. So the important question is: why are some kids just behaving immaturely?

Accommodation in Groups

Groups are breeding grounds for actions of ADHD, so children often have cooperative issues when they have to work in groups. Individuals are usually less important in group settings than the group as a whole, and they may feel neglected relative to one-on-one encounters, where they have more power and significance. Therefore, it does not come as a surprise that one-on-one communication results in less ADHD activity relative to a child being part of a group. This is why, when he started pre-school or kindergarten, your son might have been doing all right.

If the child feels ignored or rejected in a family, actions with ADHD can be quite effective in getting people back to him. ADHD activity also becomes likely when he fears that he can meet team demands. He can fall out of the operation and start taping and fidgeting. He quickly distracts the entire group from doing the operation, and somebody has to stop him from being a nuisance. While the behaviors are difficult for the person in charge, the advantages are clear.

The Basic Solution

Creating appropriate approaches to conflicts of interest is critical. Everything will be better when you and your child are considerate towards each other, and everyone is more likely to be calm and happy. For example, if your child learns to look out his friend's house window when it's time for you to pick him up, you won't mind letting him play, and you'll be happy to pick him up. You'll find the process quicker because you won't have to park the car and ring the bell to get it.

If your child learns to show greater empathy for others, the chances of success will improve. To his students, family, romantic partners, and colleagues, his loving actions will work well. It's never easy to find a compromise between self-interest and empathy for others, but it's an important skill that every parent can teach their child and a great way to eradicate ADHD behavior.

Benefits and Side Effects

ADHD activity obviously creates a lot of annoyances. It puts kids at odds with others and brings about failure. So why do kids keep doing these things because they contribute to so many harmful effects and hardships?

The reason is that while there are side effects, there are advantages that are true for most of our activities. Choosing to save instead of spend, for instance, will brace you for a comfortable retirement, but in the meantime make you less happy. Choosing to read instead of exercise may make you more knowledgeable, but may contribute to health issues. You may not have enough time to do something fun to satisfy your commitments. And when others do things for you, you might like it but hate the loss of control that happens when others make all the decisions.

Likewise, once the child shows ADHD activity in schoolwork, his grades can drop, but he also prevents the challenge of investing energy and still "falls short." In the meantime, he may also mobilize a lot of concern from educators and other important adults. The infant may not directly say no to the education and socialization challenges — as someone who may be against or defiant— but nevertheless does not comply.

The conduct of ADHD here is typically very positive. It gets others to help and lower their expectations for your child. When allowed, actions will govern to the degree that it is difficult for others to enforce any restriction or order.

Do Parents Cause ADHD Behavior?

Some parents ask, "If the behavior of ADHD is enhanced, does this mean that I have exacerbated the behavior of my child with ADHD?" The reason is that the conduct of ADHD is not the fault of anyone. Saying that there is a worsening of ADHD activity does not mean that something is wrong with you or anyone else. There are usually a lot of factors in play.

Parents do not cause behavior with ADHD, TV and video games do not cause ADHD behavior, and our society does not cause behavior with ADHD. If you put a group of people in exactly the same environment, they would show a lot of different reactions and learning patterns. The world does not entirely decide what people are doing. When working under very similar conditions, people often react and benefit in very different ways.

For example, in an attempt to get him to comply, a parent or teacher confronts a child who is upset and does not do his schoolwork. However, if the child highly values any kind of adult attention— even negative attention— this adult response may, counter-intuitively, strengthen the distracting behavior.

That's not the intention of the parent— the adult is trying to stop the action of ADHD in a manner that could potentially have the desired effect with another child.

So it's unreasonable to say that the problem is caused by the individual.

Is ADHD Behavior On Purpose?

Saying that ADHD conduct is improved does not mean that your child is actually aware of the benefits of his acts, has a sense of control over his behavior, or wants to show ADHD behavior. They may not expect to get direct responses from others or even be conscious of what usually happens when others experience activity with ADHD.

Individuals are often unaware of the interventions associated with their actions, and they sometimes work with professionals to help them learn to behave appropriately. This usually takes a lot of effort to figure out why we are doing the stuff we are doing. Your child may not know what reinforces the actions of his ADHD, just as you may not know what you can do to avoid the reinforcing.

Proceeding without Blame

A psychological understanding of the behavior of ADHD does not imply a blame for someone. Based on the child, actions of a parent can lead to very different outcomes, and related activities of children can affect parents in a wide variety of ways. For both of you, a method of learning is a dynamic process. The product of many different factors coming together is what happens over time, and the combination of participants has a lot to do with the outcomes.

Identifying the advantages of the behavior for your child is your job and then helping him to learn better alternatives. And I'm going to help you do that. You haven't caused the ADHD behavior of your child, but you can do something about it. What he learns can be influenced and help his ADHD behavior to subside over time. Really young children at risk of actions with ADHD will benefit from parental strategies in amazing ways, and that's what you'll do.

BIOLOGICAL CAUSALITY

The evidence that supports an ADHD biological cause is not as effective as it seems first. The whole view is based on three findings of the research. First, mutations have been identified by experts that increase the risk of ADHD. Second, as opposed to others, people diagnosed with ADHD have different brain biology. Third, the drug, which changes biology, often instantly eliminates the troubling behaviors. Such results sound remarkable, but let's look at each one more closely.

Genetics

The first element of the biological claim is that its ADHD is induced by the inherited nature of your child. Researchers claim that genes raise ADHD's risk by 50%. While this may seem impressive, these numbers may be deceptive. A 50 percent increase means that if the child has certain genes, the risk of ADHD will rise from 9 percent to 13.5 percent. That small increase is hardly a reason to believe that when a child has a specific genetic structure, ADHD is imminent.

In addition, the genetic account is quite small. Most individuals who are not diagnosed with ADHD have the ADHD-related hereditary structure. Some individuals with ADHD who do not have the suspicious mutations are also diagnosed. Although it is tempting to think that when chromosomes contribute to the disorder, we are finding the underlying cause of ADHD, the answer is incomplete.

Sure, when a person has specific genes, there is a small increase in risk, but much will happen along the way to change how the child will actually qualify for the diagnosis of ADHD. For example, the goal is to recognize the causes that can affect the child's ADHD behavior, regardless of what kind of genetics he has.

Brain Differences

The second aspect of the biological point of view is that people with ADHD tend to have differences in their brains compared to people without ADHD. Most experts believe this means that due to these biological differences, ADHD exists. Nevertheless, it is not the same connection or interaction as causation. Such results do not inform us whether ADHD behavior is triggered by biological differences or whether they are the effects of long-term ADHD actions. That is, such individuals ' behavior will affect their brain physiology production in measurable ways.

The lifestyle of an individual can affect brain chemistry, brain function, and the size of some parts of the brain. For example, if your child plays a musical instrument, the brain may grow differently. Therefore children living with ADHD may use biofeedback to change their brain processing habits and alertness. It means that the activity of the brain is malleable, not constant or fixed. This characteristic is termed neuroplasticity, and it is exhibited in large quantities by very young children (including those with ADHD).

If your child is often unenthusiastic when asking questions from him, those replies are likely to affect the alertness of his brain. If others solve problems for him often, the frontal lobes, the region of the brain which controls problem solving and complicated decision-making, will have less growth. When, as he responds aggressively, he always gets his way, his brain will respond and develop differently than if he had not been reinforced in that way. However, professionals searching for internal biological causes often overlook these kinds of daily experiences.

The Power of Medication

The third and final premise of the psychological claim is that in the case of ADHD, medication works because it corrects an incompetent body problem. While most people taking ADHD medications get a performance boost from them, the general public and many experts claim the drugs are successful because they compensate for some kind of genetic failure, just as insulin injections benefit people with diabetes. The medicines alter the genetics, and they believe that the source of the problem must be a flawed biology.

But with that interpretation, there are problems. Alcohol may help a person become friendlier, for instance, but that doesn't tell us why he wasn't social. Aspirin may support a person with migraine, but that doesn't tell us why he's got a headache. Radiation can help a person with cancer, but it doesn't convince us he has a deficit in radiation. The argument is that the medication may not tell us a lot about the problem's origin.

A New Way to Understand Biology and ADHD

As you may already know, children diagnosed with ADHD are more likely to experience developmental delays, movement difficulties, serious speech and language issues, complications of education, brief periods of concentration, elevated levels of activity, and frequent and demanding and intense infant responses. There is no ambiguity here for those who accept that ADHD is a genetic lag. They know we need a capable body to function effectively, and we believe that children with ADHD are not working effectively because they have less qualified brains.

This perspective may seem rational, but other views are likely. One is that problem traits, and dysfunctions can occur with ADHD because children with specific difficulties are more likely to learn behaviors with ADHD. For example, if success is impossible, a child may be less motivated to participate. Through his own initiative, he may not think he can meet standards and may become discouraged or stop trying. He may also have to rely on his parents and may find it difficult if they are not readily available.

Parents may also be less inclined to promote the independence and self-discipline of their child when their child is challenging, needy, or at risk. You would be more inclined to focus on the kid and assume responsibility for the leadership. Once these experiences occur, the self-regulatory abilities of the child can delay even further. There may be a downward spiral, generating an even stronger need for loved ones to make up for and take over.

Biology specifically causes learning effects. If a kid is very small and uncoordinated, professional basketball is impossible to ever play. There's no "football gene" he's missing; it's just that people learn different behaviors when they have different genetics styles. It is likely that the short, uncoordinated boy would avoid playing hoops and spend his time doing something that he is better at and more likely to find enjoyable.

It is not surprising that ADHD exists in families and tends to have a genetic basis, as shown in studies showing that if one identical twin has an ADHD diagnosis, the other will most likely have. We expect members of the family to show similar behavior. Family members tend to have similar bodies and backgrounds, so in similar ways, they are likely to learn. We are likely to experience equal kinds of problems and successes, and this is nowhere more true than in the case of identical twins.

So what's the conclusion?

High levels of activity, short spans of attention, and demanding and intense emotional responses all correlate with a possible diagnosis of ADHD. Early signs of maladaptive behavior are likely to interrupt childhood-wide social interaction and affect education. Whether you're a biological parent or an adoptive parent doesn't matter; these conditions make socializing a child challenging for anyone and offer fertile ground for ADHD behavior.

Instead of thinking about ADHD as a psychological problem, you should think of it as a way of working in the environment. Specific types of genetics will improve your child's chances of learning to act in an ADHD manner, but the result is not obvious. You can do much to discourage ADHD behavior even if the child has the disorder correlated with the types of early-occurring behavioral issues.

He stresses, for example, that highly active kids will benefit from a lot of stimuli. This can significantly reduce their accelerated discovery activity levels and habits. Please note that not all aggressive children are diagnosed with ADHD. When your child grows and develops, a lot can happen. There are no genetic characteristics or early performance issues that inevitably lead to a diagnosis of ADHD. And some children with ADHD, without developmental problems, start out as happy babies.

Chapter 3
The Five Reinforcements for ADHD Behavior

Obviously, very young children are self-centered. They are weak, and for protection and assistance, they rely on others. It is important to their life to be able to command the attention of their caregivers. For many hyperactive or impulsive habits, they also need reinforcement: these behaviors usually draw people and make things happen fast.

As children grow older, it is expected that they will have more control over themselves and will follow many rules. They continue to chafe their actions at these restrictions. This is when inattention can be exacerbated as a way of avoiding accountability for "big kid."

In other words, actions with ADHD (hyperactivity, impulsiveness, inattentiveness) can lead to outcomes that relieve the distress of your infant. They can also get you and others to pay more attention and support to your child. When you understand what strengthens the behavior of ADHD, you can change the effects of this kind of behavior to reduce its frequency. You will help your child learn different habits with less negative side effects, which produce better outcomes.

The Five "A"s

The ADHD behavior of your child may have any of the following beneficial effects: it may attract attention for her, it may get others to accommodate her, it may help her avoid certain situations, it may help her to acquire something she wants, and it may antagonize others to do things she doesn't like. The frequency of ADHD behavior can be increased by any of the five "A"s. These reinforcements sometimes even work in combination to drive specific behaviors, reinforcing them much more.

Attention

As soon as you start talking to a friend, your child may become rambunctious. This may happen because your relationship with someone else leads your child to become nervous. They can continue to target things off-limit or make a noise as soon as your attention shifts away from her. Such habits have the important effect of making you know what they're doing. Sometimes a familiar expression or facial movement is all it takes to allow her to attempt to replicate this form of ADHD activity.

Behaviors of ADHD can be effective ways to keep the child centered. When she is busy, hyperactive, insane, annoying or distracting, it's hard to separate from your daughter. It can be an effective way to get your mind to move by putting items next to your head or flopping randomly on your lap while you speak to someone.

Off-task activities can attract a lot of attention at school or at home. If your daughter is flounding, fiddling, or not following instructions, others may feel compelled to contact her and remain with her until she complies. This can reassure her that other people are concerned about her and that they care about her. Her neglect may lead to support and motivational opportunities, and she may like it when a person repeats her name or pleads for an answer. Her acts can even win her a seat next to you or her instructor.

Waiting rooms and other public spaces is a fertile ground for activity that attracts publicity because your child has a captive audience. This ADHD behavior will start quickly if you read a magazine to pass the time. Your daughter isn't mean; she just keeps you involved. There are many drawbacks to being loud and crazy. The one that is most noticed is often the loudest and most bizarre person in the room. Shouting can be a way to increase the probability of a response; clowning can be amusing, and when others listen, it is generally harder for parents to impose restrictions.

People might say your child can't "hold back" as well as others, but we can't ignore the effects of intense behaviors. This is definitely more apparent when the child is talking and thinking aloud. The constant chatter stops them from feeling lonely, and when you hear a running joke, you already wonder what she's doing. Her talk and noise stream keeps you both connected. She may go off on tangents, but there's no room for anyone else to talk about her never-ending story.

The tension created by action that creates publicity leaves little room for others. This doesn't necessarily mean your child doesn't get enough attention. This simply means that treatment is important, and some kids like more support than other kids do. Typically, practical jokes and multiple transgressions at school will make your child the hot topic when the family gets together later in the day. And working against your desires will guarantee that she is at the forefront of your concerns.

Accommodation

ADHD behavior usually remits as long as the child hears the word "yes." Upon hearing a child whine or create problems, loved ones will often provide comfort. This can happen when your child is overreacting, displaying anger, being self-critical, or engaging in any number of ways suggesting anxiety. When a child is diagnosed with ADHD and is considered impaired, the adults in their lives tend to lower their aspirations and offer support.

ADHD activity also leads to social housing. For example, if your child creates a scene because she wants you to leave, when you hurry along, you will unwittingly strengthen her impatience. If your child forces you to get something special to calm her down, the effect of her poor behavior is that she gets more. Even if you're threatening to punish, until you spend extra time and energy, she's still learning not to comply. ADHD will work very well to get you to give more, do more, and work harder.

Another example of this problem occurs when your child is inattentive and then relies on you to tell her what's going on. She doesn't learn to take care of herself. She's unlikely to succeed if she does this at school. Her teachers won't have the time to get her up to speed constantly.

Your child may relate love to rescue as well. If she moves into difficult or dangerous circumstances, your attempts to keep her from harm will remind her that she is valuable to you. And this involves testing so advising her of her basic needs for self-care.

The accommodated kid often asks questions about things she can easily solve on her own. She loves the fact that in order to answer her problems, you abandon everything. Playing stupid or dumb will raise assistance because it's hard to enforce conditions, keep her accountable, or encourage her to help if you have concerns about her performance. Her ineffectiveness will leave you concerned about her, and overcoming her trials and tribulations is your duty. She also complains, "Why have you not told me?" when you didn't interfere with her. When you and others "pick up the slack," the side effect is that she's unqualified.

If your daughter is used to being the focus of your needs and worries, at the detriment of others, she may learn to be self-gratifying. She is unable to adjust to what others desire if she is used to constant pampering. Showering her with easements over the course of the day or doing a lot with small milestones (such as going into the bathroom) might make it difficult for her to function in situations where accommodation is less available.

All this suggests that it is unlikely that ADHD activity can diminish as long as social housing is extreme. As in Paul's case, a child with ADHD behavior will take over a family.

Paul's Story

Paul was unable to accept or acknowledge the attempts made to please him by his family. They wanted desperately to be good parents because they came from families who were expecting a lot of them. They worked hard to please their family, and they worked hard to please Paul. Yet Paul wasn't going to let them know he was satisfied. He didn't want to feel obliged to give them up, and when he had a scowl on his face, his parents worked harder. In making them feel like losers, Paul maintained control of his family, and he wouldn't let them off the hook. He was irritable and aggressive with his younger brother when Paul was dissatisfied, so his parents went to great lengths to make sure he wasn't upset. He would sabotage an activity on some occasions that did not meet his expectations, and his parents would scurry around to make things better.

They were often concerned with him all day long. They also structured their lives in order not to bother him. Despite their best efforts to make him happy, he continued to complain and pout, and he learned that his parents would cave to make him stop. Once his parents reached the end of their wits and called out to him, he behaved as a victim; then at the end of the day, his parents felt ashamed for losing their coolness.

Unfortunately, when other people did not cater to him as his parents did, Paul experienced significant disappointment, and when he started school, this became a big problem. His hot temper and inability to adapt in that environment didn't make people bent over to accommodate him— those habits caused him endless trouble. He was not adequately prepared to function in a classroom environment because he was accustomed to significant accommodations at home. He had not yet managed to persist, avoid deceit, or make an effort to keep others satisfied.

Not surprisingly, Paul decided not to do his assignments. He would often leave unfinished assignments and projects, and it took him hours to complete a small school task. His parents sat with him and did much of the work for him in an effort to keep him from failing, and to calm the drama.

While Paul enjoyed the fact that he was able to get his parents to shoulder most of his homework, this situation's downside is evident: he did not meet expectations on his own. Only because his parents worked so hard he received passing grades. His parents certainly wanted to help him, but he also learned many behaviors that were consistent with an ADHD diagnosis.

Why Parents Over Accommodate

For many reasons, parents can frequently make accommodations on their child's behalf. Sometimes parents feel that not protecting the child is too dangerous. Parents are likely to err on the safe side if parents are worried about potential risks. They are also more inclined to compromise if they are susceptible to shame. In particular, single parents may over-accommodate because of guilt because the child has been through a divorce because they feel they have neglected the child because they have worked too many hours, or because the child has experienced the other parent's abandonment. For their own poverty as children, some parents are eager to please their child. These parents don't want to suffer as their child has suffered. Some are more suitable to ease the pain of a traumatized child. They solve problems carefully so the kid is not going to have to experience unnecessary challenges or threats. Some may do too much for their child because they are in a rush and have no time to let the child learn from their own mistakes. Some are concerned that they are not strong enough, and they are too happy to be admitted. And some take over most of the family burden as they had to do that when they grew up. Whatever the cause or excuse, compromise will conflict with a child's self-management growth and ability to meet other people halfway.

We may all want to make things easier for our kids, but kids also need to learn that fighting is part of life. The difficulty, of course, is to strike a balance between too much expectation and too little settlement. While you may build a relationship with your daughter by doing something appealing to her, you may be promoting actions that won't let her work without your feedback. As parents, we may like it when our kids feel close to us, safe and cared for, but we also want them to develop self-reliance so that when we're not around, they can do for themselves.

When you simplify a project or give your child hints to a solution before making a reasonable attempt, you are helpful, but she does not want to exert herself. When you ask her to take her things, without your reminder, she may not learn to recall them. And if you're eager to help her with her dress, it certainly saves time and makes things easier, but you also prolong the moment she decides to properly put on her hat. In fact, you will build quite a strain for yourself and grow up in the future to hate this structure.

Avoidance

To children and adults alike, avoidance is a very common way to cope with adversity. Avoidance benefits can perpetuate distractibility and lack of focus and listening, which are the hallmarks of ADHD's. Like Mark Twain says, "Staying out is easier than getting out." However, we don't achieve control because we ignore it, and the question never goes away. In the end, it is not safe for any of us to hide our heads in the sand like an ostrich.

Once a child is diagnosed with ADHD, most people no longer attempt to understand the actions of the child as an inability to cooperate, attend, or adapt. They conclude that when we talk to her, her ADHD stops her from paying attention. They think she can't learn to stop and listen to what you're doing. If she continues to play and fails to respond to your demands, they presume it is because she is hyper-focused pathologically. People will stop saying she hates you; they will blame her lack of courtesy and sensitivity on her ADHD instead.

But all these distracted responses also have benefits. These can often protect your daughter from danger and encourage her to move on with her mission. She may feel others are not listening to her, so in return, she stops listening. This includes tuning out or yawning at others when they're critical or demanding. It involves changing the topic when they press her to discuss certain topics. And it involves daydreaming, and not acknowledging others.

Instead of having an inability, your child may have discovered that she doesn't have to adhere to the condition you enforce if she doesn't react. Distractibility gives her more time to do what she wants. It allows her to float away on her imagination.

Distractibility prevents an child from pain of all sorts. It takes her away from assessment, punishment, and restriction-related conditions. Her absorption in her own thinking and actions saves her from distasteful things, like too simple or repetitive activities.

As soon any she feels you're nagging or lecturing, your child may also become lethargic, and a weary expression can sweep over her eyes. Many people know how hard it is to listen to extended speech without getting a chance to get feedback. If the speech goes on long enough, many people may start showing up under arousal, and their brain biology will reflect how they respond. Such sorts of responses are shown very often and very rapidly in children with ADHD.

Your child may seem incapable, distracted, and unfocused, but she's also avoiding what disrupts her and hiding, so she doesn't have to hear anything negative about herself or probably feel a sense of disappointment. When she feels she must be flawless or believes other people will be appreciative, she may be even less likely to immerse herself and stay on the job. In such situations, the slightest noise in the room may catch her interest, though it would go unnoticed at other times — when she is relaxed with what she does.

Perhaps your daughter often doesn't understand what she's just learned. But if she doesn't find pleasure in what she's hearing (or if she's thinking about something else), it's normal if she drifts away looking at the phrases. And maybe when she says she is unable to focus, you will stop reproaching her and pushing her to participate completely in this kind of boring task, because then your attempts will seem futile.

It can also be signs of stress and a desire to escape fidgeting with objects and squirming. Such actions also mean that a child is perturbed by what is going on and needs to get away. She might insist she can't stay in her place, but sitting in the corner and taking her pencil forever to sharpen helps her to postpone the job she doesn't want to do for a long time.

Not arranging their resources and missing tasks will increase the play time of your child. She stops putting things aside from the extra work and sidesteps unwelcome activities. She actually learns new ways of evading if you challenge her. When you challenge her to listen, she can chat or move, and you can't get a word in edgewise.

The habits that we call "impulsive" may also be correlated with avoidance. For example, she may cause a commotion by doing something impetuous when she is disturbed. Not only does she get to let go of steam, but she also distracts herself successfully from what upset her.

A similar benefit occurs when your child is wandering around, rambles, and entertains. Although attentiveness is triggered by actions, they often divert us from what was happening. This can reduce family feuds or uncomfortable silences efficiently. The behavior of your child will help bring down the level of stress.

Acquisition

Many actions of ADHD allow a child to get things faster. The "Strike while the iron is hot" proverbs and "Take it while you can" demonstrate the advantages of urgent action. Often the kid who behaves quickly won't miss out, because it's hard for others to block swift and aggressive goal-oriented actions, such as moving forward to get the biggest piece of cake. Some ADHD behaviors will discourage others from refusing what they want to deny to your child. If her acts are sudden, your daughter will easily get what she wants, and she doesn't stop giving her change to others.

If children pick, harass inappropriately, behave rudely, act recklessly, or inflict on others, we don't like it, but when they work so well, it's hard to get these habits to end. Your child will ping-pong around the house in search of some form of excitement, just as you do while channeling surfing. Generally, ADHD actions will speed things up and break side barriers to help your child find pleasure quicker. Impulsive behavior makes it hard for others to predict their decisions and prevent them from getting what they want.

Your child may also gain a sense of prestige by blurring out what others are afraid to say. It's not that she lacks a filter; it's that if you like it or not, her acts enhance her effect. They try to encourage respectful behavior, but sometimes when she's impolite, a child loses out less often, and sometimes it's better to say "sorry" than to ask for permission. They may think the child lacks the ability to delay gratification or worry about it before she behaves, but it's just her ADHD behavior that works too well.

Your daughter should enjoy the fun of getting what she wants, even if negative consequences will come down the line. The acts become even more valuable when others save or the smooth things out when there are future problems. It is therefore important to determine how often people save her before concluding that her rashness is a symptom of illness.

Antagonism

She might want to strike back when your child is angry or upset. While some children fight for themselves assertively or actively, in reaction to confrontation, children living with ADHD are usually more subtle. They could, for example, flip small objects in your face or play with a household item recklessly. We call them impulsive actions, but they serve a purpose. They leave you very annoyed, and that's just good for the kids.

In this situation, the bigger the response to actions— the more exasperated and frustrated you are — the more likely the behavior will be replicated. Your child will learn precisely how to "push your buttons." For instance, once your child becomes upset that he is expected to wait for an appointment, his humiliating actions will threaten you. While you may think she's blurring out because she can't control her impulses, it's not at all. Her acts are powerful ways you can be depressed by pulling her along.

It's not that she's having trouble "putting on the brakes." If she makes a scene, she baits and disrupts you. She will flail around and touch over and over again what you forbid her to touch. All these acts can be irritating, and they can serve as revenge. She knows you're disturbed by your unruliness before others, so she makes you mindful of yourself because you don't want to be seen as a bad parent.

Why Does Your Child Antagonize?

The replies I've just given indicate outstanding relationship issues. It is crucial to identify and solve these problems if your parenting is to be effective. You want your child to be successful in dealing with disappointment and conflict. Antagonism is just keeping the feud going.

Nevertheless, your child may not always know what is bothering her. By realizing what she's upset with, she might be instigating and upsetting, and you might not realize either. She may not be angry at all with you at times. She might take her frustrations out on you because you're either "safe" or the first one available. She might sometimes antagonize you simply because you didn't give her attention or refused to make a request.

Identifying motives for antagonism of a child is not always easy. Relationships can be complex and hard to untangle. Some circumstances that trigger memories of old incidents and interfere with your child's current relationship.

Overreacting the child may sometimes mean that on more than one occasion, the issue has arisen. To deal with things that keep repeating, it's difficult for anyone, and your child may also overreact at these moments. For instance, if it has been an ongoing issue between you, she may become intolerable because she feels you mean that she is untrustworthy.

Your child may also be antagonistic to you when she feels you are unwilling to include her. Her irritating behavior can be a way of gaining dominance, avoiding the risk of being nice and becoming disappointed afterwards. She can retaliate if she feels unwelcomed by doing something disrespectful. This will pressure you to adapt and cause you to fail in the process. We all know that "misery loves company." Your child can do the hurting, rather than feeling teased and weak. She controls the rejection when you're bothered or disgusted. Antagonizing can help her feel less fragile, and it can check whether you care enough to overcome her unhappiness and make her settle down.

Antagonizing can also be disguised and roundabout. Your child may tell you she is going to complete an assignment, but then she is not going to complete it. She may poorly perform the assignment, lose it, or not turn it in. Many children who have been diagnosed with ADHD quietly fight by failing to do what is important to their parents, including schoolwork and household duties. Their weapon is failing, and they can act out the worst fears of their parents. Usually, though, the battle leads to nothing positive. Your child is getting less and endangered, while you are becoming more and more distressed.

A Frequent Benefit

You may wonder if your child could profit from all this fighting. But the most important and frequent advantage of antagonism is the subsequent make-up. You may regret, for instance, that you overreacted and feel like you owe an apology to your son. This may include pleasing and accommodating her in ways that otherwise would not happen. Since misbehaving, your daughter may also want to patch things up, and you may need to interrupt what you're doing to attend to her forgiving request. As with most ADHD habits, the effect is that the kid enjoys time and energy dominance.

Your daughter may be hesitant to forgive you on some days, though, which may add to your attempt to please her even more. You may want to comfort her from other family members, and she may hope to receive consolation by convincing them you are unkind. If your child comes to you for help, think about your reaction. Could it perpetuate antagonistic behavior? Unfortunately, if others comfort her, they will undoubtedly undermine your disciplinary attempts. Even though events started creating what seemed to be unnecessary trouble with your child, they ended with the tables turned completely.

Everybody thinks your mistake is the problem. No wonder it's hard to eliminate the actions of ADHD.

Identifying Frequent Triggers

It is important that you look closely at the past experiences of your child so that you can figure out what has reinforced her ADHD behavior over time. Understand that, given its history, the effects of ADHD actions for your child may be more damaging than for others. There is no clear context that describes any form of ADHD behavior, even though we see trends. Even very different stories can cause ADHD behavior and intensify it. For example, a feeling of entitlement may lead to the intrusiveness of a child, but a child who would otherwise be left out or neglected may also experience intrusiveness. A child can demonstrate delayed self-management either with diligent parents who take care of everything or with careless, hasty, and disorganized parents. Which issue or problems can underlie the actions of your child?

ADHD activity has a wide range of possible causes. Three common ones are perceived as incompetence insinuations, a feeling of inferiority, and parents who are depleted.

Perceived Insinuations of Incompetence

A child may react to the influence and oversight of a parent as if this action indicates that the child is incompetent. The child may not understand the parent's concern about security and trying to be supportive. The child might wonder why the adult is so constantly controlling and directing her acts. She might think the parent is trying to control her or taking away her decision-making opportunities. The parent may be accused of treating her as a baby.

The child may take on more than she can handle and make more mistakes in an attempt to prove the parent wrong, resulting in her parent hovering and directing her actions more. Her response to her parent exacerbates the problem. As the cycle continues, she that become more and more non-responsive to suggestions in her protest. Her search to avoid the parent is through efforts by the parent to stop her. In the meantime, the behavior of ADHD is triggered, and the trend is the norm.

A Feeling of Inferiority

A child may also see herself as inferior and incompetent at other moments. She can believe that she is not as qualified as her sibling, who can outwit and outperform her in most cases. Her tensions may be building up, and she may sidestep criteria to avoid exposing her incompetence. She may argue that all the good attention is paid to her parent, and she may see herself as a loser. She avoids playing with the star in the family instead of trying and probably losing, instead gaining attention with a number of ridiculous activities.

This does not mean that ADHD is triggered by capable parents. Most children with capable parents have no activity with ADHD. The point is that competent siblings, in ways that increase ADHD behavior, can affect specific children.

Depleted Parents

If a parent doesn't feel good, the enthusiasm of a child may be daunting. Whenever a parent is mentally drained, the parent is more likely to retreat, become irritable, or give in to the pestering of a child to immediately ease the situation. For example, if a parent sits in the bedroom until things get messy, a child can learn to be loud and disruptive in a variety of ways.

Depleted parents may increase the likelihood of activity with ADHD because they respond more frequently in ways that reinforce it.

Although not all children can respond to a stressed mother with ADHD behavior, whenever there is impatience, anxiety, and lack of discipline and follow-up, the way a child learns to self-manage and communicate with others is likely to have an impact. ADHD behavior can work to the benefit of the child by making the parent more powerless and more attention-causing. And it can be a way of avoiding or antagonizing someone who feels nervous.

Chapter 4

Teaching Your Child SELF-CARE

Our starting point is to improve the self-care of your child. You will, of course, have help if needed, but if she manages to handle her self-care independently, it will be beneficial to her. Because if she is eager to be self-reliant, she will be more likely to follow through, the strategies in this chapter are intended to foster her enthusiasm.

It is better if your child learns to carry out self-care in response to signs in her surroundings while gaining autonomy, rather than dependent on your verbal instruction. For example, teach her to wake up to an alarm clock instead of your voice. Always, remember to consider your daughter as successful: believe she will learn to put toothpaste on her own toothbrush, pour her own glass of milk, use a watch, choose her own shoes, and dress alone. Even very young children can perform these kinds of things, and with your child, you can assume the same.

Your child may not have an age-appropriate accountability background. According to study, children living with ADHD in their self-management skills are on average 30 percent behind other children. Unless you tell your child to wash after using the bathroom, pick up after herself, brush her teeth, unzip her jacket, etc., she may not do these things and do little self-care. But why doesn't she know these basic rituals and habits?

Emphasizing the Advantages

If you try to teach your child self-care, she may be able to respond negatively to your efforts. She may feel like you're pulling away, pushing her to do more work, and taking away your time and companionship. When that happens, she may be balking at the important thing to do; the self-care.

As with weaning, parental efforts to encourage their self-care are pushing away many children. Children are reluctant to give up the support provided by family, so children risk rejection because their parents are not interested in every detail of their lives. They may be worried that any self-sustaining behavior, particularly their siblings, will encourage their parents to concentrate on other issues.

If you suspect this is the case, ask your child the rhetorical question, "If you took better care of yourself, do you think I'd forget about you?" also say,' I wonder if you'd like to grow up with me more,' and imagine what you could do together.

Help your child understand the self-reliance advantages. For example, without you, she can go more places, others won't harp on her so often, and she can perform tasks when there's no help available. You want her to know that when she displays good self-care, she will benefit more than she loses. The words you use and your voice tone will affect whether she's responding positively, and it's always helpful to note her self-care growth and willingness to help others.

Helping Your Child Follow Through Independently

Helping your daughter do what she says she's going to do without having to remind her is vital. Scientists have built a way to help people with their plans to follow through. In this special way, if you help your child "planning for success," there is an increased chance that she will carry out her plan immediately on her own.

Ask your child to tell you what she's going to do and define when, where, and how she's going to do it as if she'd been rehearsing for a play. Then have her recognize the stimuli that will alert her to enforce her strategy in the area. You should step aside by making her focus on the setting to guide her. Since she takes the lead, she is also expected to be better in her determination to follow through.

This strategy may have amazing results. For example, if your daughter wants to remember bringing back a library book at the end of the week, she will decide to put the book next to her musical instrument that she always takes to school for the rehearsal of Friday group. This will allow her to see the book on that day before she leaves the house, which will signify her return.

POOR HYGIENE

You may keep reminding your child to brush or shower, but this may not be the best solution for you. Also, if your child depends on your efforts, she's not going to learn how to handle it on her own. Also, she will resent the constant reminder and believe you doubt her ability.

Your child knows you're agonizing about her grooming, so failing to meet your expectations could turn into a powerful weapon to threaten you when she's upset. In addition, if she likes the fact that you're worried about her, she might also be reluctant to give up. Kids are often told that when they overreact to grooming problems, their parents care for them.

There may be many different reasons for the failure of a child to perform the simple self-care routines. Here are some examples.

- Robert was affected by poor modeling; his parents preserved their grooming by copying the mediocre style.
- Fine motor problems clashed with Michael's self-care; he suffered more than others did, and his parents got accustomed to taking control of themselves.
- Philip felt safer when his body smell kept others at the length of his arm.

Identifying what is hampering the child in this field is important. Fortunately, children do not always see sanitation in a negative light. For starters, when they get in, kids are often hesitant to get out of the shower. An inability to begin a hygiene-related project seems to have very little to do with the negative operation.

Solutions

Negative words and coercion can often have a detrimental effect on the hygiene response of your child, and this is often a factor in resistance. Checking to see if she washed her hands with soap, or asking her to use it, will only render hand washing an unpleasant activity she would hate. If you experience a power struggle to wash your hands, then you might ask her: "What's going on? Are you all right when you let germs live on your paws, or are you upset when you like I'm running you around?" Being positive, maintaining the pleasure and complimenting the expertise of your child will encourage her to be clean.

Now let's concentrate on brushing of teeth as an example. When she wants to take care of her teeth and figure out when she wants to clean them, you should ask your daughter. When she has a recommendation, you may say, "After every meal, the dentist says to clean them. This keeps the teeth healthy and strong.

Avoid perpetuating dependency on your child. Instead of brushing the teeth of your child, teach her how to do it. Ask, "I can show you how the dentist taught me." Help her recognize that when she manages her hygiene, she takes good care of herself. Healthy teeth need less repair work (which is never quite pleasant), and when others see her good smile and note how great she looks, your child may like it.

However, sometimes your child may be testing to see if she has the right to say no to a request for hygiene, and you may recognize this problem rather than insist on it. When her health is bad for a short time, the world won't end. If you don't always apply pressure, your child may be less immune. As the saying goes, "Choose your battles." The poor hygiene of your child may have little to do with failing to understand the effects of their actions. As you know, to prove a point, many people are doing all sorts of things to themselves.

If the problem persists, a reality check can make things happen. You want your daughter to know what might happen if she chooses to be careless. If Nick failed to use his orthodontic "appliance," for instance, it was important to remind him that his mistake could lead to significant jaw malformation. The mother asked, "Isn't that much worth wearing to you?" When your back is against the wall, you can always ask the question," If you don't want to, would you be willing to do it?" Most of us, after all, do things we don't want to do. Like most highly acceptable practices, conscientious self-care requires commitment to plans and other constraints whether we like it or not. We all face this inconvenience, and even when we are not head-over-heels, we know to obey. Suppose your child is able to learn to do the same.

Developing Routines

It is important for things like washing your hands and body and brushing your teeth to establish daily routines. That's how most people's health is assured. Try to help your child identify environmental signals that will remind her to brush and wash. The invite to begin a meal, for example, could signify that she washed her hands. Getting into her pajamas might give her a signal to brush her teeth. The goal, as always, is to establish a routine without you that she can do.

If your daughter doesn't do her routine, instead of spelling out each step, you might say, "It's getting late" or "We've got to leave soon." This will give her a better chance to control herself compared to telling her exactly what to do. If you notice that she missed a step in her bedtime routine — brushing her teeth— you might ask, "Is there anything else you might still like to do before you go to sleep?" You may inquire, just as a last resort," Are you sure that you want to go to bed without having to brush?"

Being Firm

Forcing a child to do hygiene does not make sense unless there is no other choice, and this will only work when she is very young and easy to physically overwhelm. Yet strict limits will improve the ability of your child to comply. For example, if she tends to ignore her teeth, you may say, "We may need to use some of our film money to pay the dentist of extra visits." If her lack of self-care still makes her vulnerable to cavities, you may add, "You might choose not to clean, but in that situation, it's probably best not to buy the treats that may be bad for your teeth."

You don't try to make your child suffer, you protect her, don't threaten her. You are determined to tackle a problem and take firm action, whether it upsets her or not. The approach makes her understand that, as well as herself, her failure impacts others.

Ostracizing

You may find it necessary to ostracize your daughter in some extreme circumstances to overcome her lack of hygiene. Because it's necessary to be considerate of others, you might suggest, "We'd love to have you join us, but only if you're able to shower and get ready in clean clothes." If she keeps refusing, you might ask her, "Is there any reason to create this kind of family problem? Were you distracted by something else?" If there is no improvement, and if it is possible for someone to live with her at home when you go out, you might leave your child behind. We should think about how this will impact the family budget if you have to hire someone to monitor her. You may allow her to pay the sitter with her personal money (or sell some of her toys if she doesn't have cash). Yes, she has the power to sabotage, but she misses the excursion as well and helps with her personal funds to offset the inconvenience. She then decides whether hygiene should be disregarded.

DIFFICULTIES WITH DRESS

Your child is likely to have packing, buttoning, and zipping issues, so it's crucial for her to learn those skills. She might not be enthusiastic about giving up your help, unfortunately. For examples, she might yell out "Ma!" And then lift her leg nonchalantly and wait until you put it on her sock. You can feel negligent if you don't support her, but by providing such assistance, you don't perpetuate laziness or superiority.

Alternatively, just offer enough help to keep advancing slowly. Unless you offer assistance as soon as your daughter cries or says, "I can't," her abilities in self-care will fail. Asking her to explain that she is unable to do is a constructive first move that will keep the ball in her hands.

Solutions

It takes time to help your child develop self-help skills. If you're hurried and pressured to get things done, you're not going to have the luxury of waiting for her to solve and improve problems. She may doubt that she can learn to meet expectations quickly enough, and she may be disrupted and discouraged. When you prepare, this dilemma can be eliminated, and things can work better. For starters, the night before, when there's time to work together, you should discuss clothing options. It beats becoming frenzied when the time is short in the morning.

If your child has more authority with her clothes, she may show more interest and cooperation as well. You might just point out, "It's cold outside," instead of telling her what to wear on a cold day. This will help her feel she has more control over her outfit selection. She can learn to check the weather herself as she gets older.

Clothing Decisions

Sometimes you may need to rely on certain clothes to protect your child against the weather or to make sure her wardrobe is suitable. But often her choices on clothes will not be too offensive to justify disciplinary intervention. Like your child's pediatrician will tell you, it's just because she's underdressed that your daughter won't catch a cold — she'll just be cold. And if she's cold enough, in the future, she'll probably make different choices. That's the strength of natural causes.

On some instances, you may be afraid that if she doesn't wear those clothes, your daughter will spoil a family outing. You may be scared that when you cannot turn back, she will become unhappy and make things difficult for others. In these cases, you may advise her to bring certain things along "just in case." It may also help to find a comfortable way to carry the extra clothes (so that she does not feel burdened). Choose a solution that is appropriate to both of you instead of demanding a solution.

Let her know when it's necessary for your daughter to dress in a certain way. For instance: "These are the kinds of clothes that we wear to the church. Which one would you like to wear today?" There are very few choices at times. There may be other reasons for her inability to comply if your child begins to scream. As with hygiene, it's not always a matter of clothes, so figure out if she's distracted by something else. That can solve just fine the problem.

Yet saying a word to your daughter doesn't mean she's having her way. For starters, if you bring home clothes, you've bought of her and she doesn't want to put them on, let her say, "I can wait until tomorrow, but then I'll have to get them back to the store." This kind of ordinary result might pique her attention and get her to test out the new clothes sooner. If you're still having trouble purchasing clothes, browse for her clothing only when she's with you.

Wearing the same outfit

If your child wants to wear the same outfit for many days in a row, it may make you feel uncomfortable. You may be worried that when you allow this to happen, you are irresponsible, and you may be worried about her grubby look and how others will react.

While the attachment of your daughter to her outfit that give you panic, ask yourself, if she appears disheveled, is it really so terrible? Is it worth quibbling about? If the answer is yes, you might say to her: "I know you really like the pants and the top. Perhaps I can wash the shirt, so it's going to last longer. I will wash the trousers for you after the top is dry. "During the cleaning process, your daughter still keeps half of the outfit with this method.

You may think your child will continue to wear dirty clothes unless you force the problem, but when you're in a power struggle, negativity and stiffness are more likely. So it's nice that she told you not to mock her and clean her hair. It is generally better to find a mutually agreeable solution.

Compliments help

Complimenting your child when she looks extraordinarily dapper is a great way to encourage competent dressing. Instead of criticizing or joking about her crazy outfits (which may encourage silliness), she does not pick acceptable outfits or color combinations, notice when she is well-coordinated. You could say, "Wow! You're looking really clean. You should know how these colors will fit.

DIFFICULTIES WITH SLEEP

Sleep is vital to the health of your child, so establishing a good sleep schedule is crucial. Getting up early every morning (with no naps during the day) will help your child get into a normal 24-hour phase called a circadian rhythm. Variations in weekend sleep schedule will make it hard for your child on Monday morning to get up for school, so try to maintain some consistency. If your child has good sleeping patterns, she will eventually learn to wake up even without an alarm at the same time every day.

Children diagnosed with ADHD often have problems with sleep. During the day, they have more episodes of sleepiness, and their lack of sleep raises their issues with conduct and school inattention. That's why figuring out what might mess with your child's sleep is very necessary.

It is important to recognize and resolve any issues that impact your child's sleep. Often a kid resists sleep just as she resists all the other restrictions you place. When you say, "You've got to sleep," she says, "Why?" So he finds a reason for saying no. Sometimes it's just a trick to get you to communicate with her. Her failure to do the routine of bedtime forces you to drop what you're doing, step into a drama and be concerned about her well-being.

Solutions

When you read the sleep treatment of Richard Ferber, you know how important it is to have your child learn to sleep without having to depend on you. In many ways, the approach you learn in this book is an extension of the Ferber method for many of your child's problems. Without your daily support and encouragement, you are teaching your child to handle life.

The first step is to set up a routine for your child to start and finish without you. Try to set up a predictable time to start the bedtime routine from the outset. You want her to stop doing other things, do laundry, and get into her pajamas so you can rest, listen, tell stories, and so on.

At first, you may provide a reminder, but pair it as soon as possible with other signals (a clock, a TV show completion, etc.). You might say, "Let's get ready for stories as soon as your show is over," but very simply, without your intervention, you want your child to adapt to signals that occur.

If your daughter avoids the schedule you've created, let her know you're ready to start bedtime activities and wait for her to do so. Mention that if she passes, you'll have more time together. It shows you that you are interested in sharing the exclusive time set aside.

Maintain Limits

While showing willingness to overcome any obstacles and being flexible when circumstances are extenuating, you want your child to realize that bedtime has a firm start and end. Your child will know that you're done when the clock strikes an hour. Beginning late means you're both going to have less time together. If the bedtime ritual is completely ignored by your daughter, you may need to escort her to her room under duress. It will help her to develop punctuality by setting firm limits.

When bedtime is over, your child comes out of her room, don't take care of her. Nor is it advisable to punish her with another consequence, such as removing television or earlier bedtime. Clearly steer her without speaking to her room. You can always ask her later, "What can we do to make your bedtime easier to end?" And, "How are you going to end your bedtime?" Help solve the issue.

Explore obstacles

It may be difficult to achieve a perfect bedtime routine; numerous issues can come to the fore. Often one parent may be disengaged, and the non-participating parent gets the argument off the sofa at bedtime. It is necessary in these cases to overcome what leads to the inability of that parent to be involved.

Older Children

When your child grows older, she's likely going to want more feedback on her bedtime. This will require more problem-solving. You want her to sleep plenty, but without feeling forced into an unpleasant thing. Often the problem is getting enough downtime to meet commitments to maintain health and get enough time to finish what she needs to do. You could say, "How much sleep do you want to have in the morning to feel good?" So," he said, "is it worth giving up your sleep to read the chapter?"

It may work better if you record the program for her to watch another day instead of allowing your child to stay up late to watch a TV program. You could also encourage her to complete school work earlier, so she has more time to enjoy herself when other family members are available later in the evening. Try to set up an overnight schedule that helps the rest of the family to have personal time and productive energy. Make sure that you have some flexibility for such a period, though, or that negative attention can increase.

Difficulty Caring for Personal Belongings

If your child wants you to pick up after her, she may not show due respect for personal belongings and care. She may throw playthings to the side without consideration to the mess she makes as soon as they annoy her, leaving a trail of her belongings throughout the building. You don't want to behave like her personal servant forever, so it's important to take responsibility for her possessions from your child.

Solutions

When you look at people who keep things quiet and dry, you'll probably notice three habits that they do regularly. First, before a mess gets unwieldy, they do some cleaning up. Second, they clean up so that the room is available for something else when they're done with an activity. Third, when they no longer need them, they return objects to their designated locations. It means the things are safe and easy to locate. It's not rocket science to stay organized. It just takes these processes to be completed.

Support her get into the habit of picking up before the chaos becomes unbearable and before starting something new as she tells your daughter to care about her belongings. Since knowing when it's appropriate to leave things out, you can ease back. Let her think, "These things were put away when you play the game." If she's left in the kitchen behind her toys, tell her, "Please come to the kitchen and take your toys."

Promoting Self-Management

If your daughter is going to take care of her personal belongings, she will give up the privilege of putting things away for her by someone else. She has to give up the advantage of having people scurry around trying to find something she can't find. And when she stops an activity that is not yet complete, she has to figure out what to do. Sometimes putting things away when there's a good reason to keep them handy is not worth it— we're all feeling this way at some point.

Those who like incredibly smooth and clean things tend towards putting things aside, even if they might eventually use them again. They don't mind the extra work, because they don't like the clutter, and they are super-protective their possessions. Nevertheless, your child may choose the contrary. She can stop the extra work, deal with the chaos, and take the opportunity when things get lost or damaged. All sides have their advantages, and a middle ground typically has the fewest pitfalls, as is evident in almost any aspect of life.

The organizational behavior of an individual may also vary depending on the importance of protecting a particular item, the cleaning challenge, and the consequences of dealing with the mess. For example, in the middle of the kitchen floor, a disheveled bedroom or playroom has more repercussions than the same untidiness. All this may sound complicated, but it means that in different circumstances, the child needs to learn different behaviors.

Set firm limits

I can guarantee that if she has too many, your daughter will be reckless with her possessions. When you replace them too quickly, she will less likely secure her possessions. If you pick up after her, she won't have any trouble with the mess she makes. While some kids are too harried or troubled to exert their energy and spend time with personal belongings to be conscientious, many expect their parents to pick up things for them. They also assume that lost items will be found or replaced by their parents. Disciplinary weakness often allows carelessness to continue.

So if you feel you are being treated like a maid or butler by your child, stand tall and stay steady. For example, if she doesn't pick up her candy wrappers, say, "I love you a lot, and I'm just a little disappointed, but I keep finding candy wrappers all over the place." Ask for her help to solve the problem, but if nothing helps, say, "I don't know what else to do, except stop buying candy until I see you pick up after yourself." You might say: "Let's place these things in storage, so you're going to have less to look at. We can add more toys if all that stuff isn't going to be such a hassle for you to deal with. "You can also let her know that leaving toys underfoot gives you the message that the toys don't matter to her. Find out, "If you don't have a better idea, I should store the toys to get them out of everybody's way." If you end up taking this step, and she protests, you could suggest something like, "They're in the attic. I thought you didn't care for them because they've been sitting there for days.

However, too much focus on cleaning up after yourself can lead to the reluctance of your child to clean up a mess unless it's done. Your daughter could learn to say, "I'm not putting it away — I haven't taken it out," because she's heard you say the same thing. In this case, you could respond that helping people sometimes doesn't encourage them to be lazy. Sometimes a mistake is not due to negligence, and if everyone joins in and lends a hand, there is no drawback.

POOR MONEY MANAGEMENT

ADHD-diagnosed children and adults have a history for irresponsibly spending money. The condition may get so serious that their family and spouses end up spending their money. While some may think that people with ADHD are unable to consider the long-term consequences of frivolous spending, there is another way to understand the problem: as with other limitations they ignore, individuals with ADHD do not accept the boundaries of money management. They are less likely to say no to their wishes. Your job, of course, is to improve your child's behavior.

Nevertheless, your child can feel powerless when it comes to money. She probably depends on you to allow her access to money, and you may find it prudent to supervise her transactions even if she has her own income. You want her to build financial responsibility and learn to save by herself, but you also want her to enjoy spending pleasure. It's not always easy to find a comfortable balance.

Without question, the experiences of your child will have an impact on their money handling. She will mirror those habits if you spend money irresponsibly. If she has an endless supply of money, she is never going to say no to a buy. She won't have any incentive to save because money seems to "grow on trees."

When you bail her out too often when she doesn't have resources, she won't learn to put money aside as well. She's going to assume you're going to reward her. And if she wants to be reliant on you, she may be poor and needy.

Help your child recognize that everyone in the family has to live within a budget to encourage sound money management: there is only a certain amount of money available for purchases. This can even be understood by very young children. She can begin to understand the principle of insufficient funds as soon as your child understands the concept of "not enough."

Personal Money

Giving personal money to a child at the age of four or five is now common practice. You can hold your child personal money and keep a record on a piece of paper so she can easily see it. It's important, to be honest, and give her the money you've earmarked without asking her for it. When you hold accurate records, it is helpful. It tells her you are trustworthy, and she starts to learn how to keep a bankbook. Because she knows how much cash she's saving, she'll know how much she can spend as well. Hand the money over to her when you know she's ready and she knows to keep it safe and organized.

Instead of allowing your child to perform a certain chore or assignment (especially for work that is not out of the ordinary), give her a reward simply because she is part of the family. That strategy removes the possible side effect that, when you give compensation, she won't help. It also makes her understand how to prioritize and spend wisely because you're going to ask her to use her own money to make those purchases (e.g. a new doll for her collection). Then you decide what type of donation you want her to make with her own funds (for example, pay half of the doll's cost).

Emphasize the members of the family usually help one another without payment. While your child's income doesn't depend on it, the family hopes she'll act considerately because that's the "family style." If she's not behaving like that, try to find out why, but don't keep subsidizing her if she's behaving egoistical and taking advantage of others.

When you believe your daughter is freeloading, it may be advisable to reduce her allowance. You can justify your actions frankly by saying, "We can use your share of money to pay someone else to help us out if you choose not to chip in." Let her know the inability to lend a hand falls on others. Make it clear; if she wanted to join, you'd like it, but it's also important to make sure the household doesn't work.

A similar problem happens when the child continues to take items from others, fails or is disruptive. Let her that you have to hold her accountable because that respects other people's rights. Say, "We need your money to help pay for the deficit," which makes her grow to be more conscientious and to try less costly ways of solving her irritability. Similarly, if she has a tendency to be reckless in a store, warn her, "Have your bankbook ready for anything that breaks."

EATING PROBLEMS

You are concerned that your child's eating can create a drama she may not want to give up. Parents with prematurely born children are continuously in this predicament. Their doctors warn them to make sure that their baby gains weight, and from day one they get into the habit of forcing the baby to eat.

Eating will easily turn into a will war. You want your child to eat well, but that needs her to make good food choices. Blocking access to food, using food as a reward or punishment, criticizing her eating behavior, using food to keep her busy, or forcing her to eat certain foods may seem to solve the surface problem. Such parenting behaviors, however, may increase overeating, sneaking food, refusing to eat, and fighting for power. You can end up contributing rather than reducing atypical eating habits.

Solutions

Make it a family tradition to sit at a table together and consider mealtime a joy for your child to be there. You don't want to make eating an uncomfortable experience. So don't force her to take some extra help or challenge her to finish all the food on her plate. When you show feeling rude or irritated when she is not involved in the food you prepare, you may create problems.

So if she's not hungry for what you've prepared, simply wrap up the food and let her know if she wants to eat it later.

Say, "What is a healthy amount for one meal, instead of condemning the amount she eats?" This approach involves her in making decisions and treats her with respect. When you think she takes too much and deprives others, ask her to help you prepare the meals and figure out how portions can be divided.

Help her understand the benefits of eating small portions of certain foods; see if in one sitting you can decide on how much to eat. You might suggest, "If you're hungry, maybe we have something healthier for you to eat." As always, the trick is to create a plan that works for you both, as you can't always control what she puts in her mouth. As the saying goes, "You can bring a horse to water, but you can't make it drink."

It can also be a way to promote healthy eating, not to bring certain foods into the house. Out of sight, out of mind. You also want to make good food choices for your child, though, even when there is unhealthy food to be taken. So instead of taking her Halloween candy from her, which means she doesn't have self-control, help her find an acceptable way to manage the sweets.

When promoting healthy nutrition, instead of suggesting, "You can't eat sweets until you eat your greens," suggest, "It's easier for us to eat these things first." Let her know, "Sweets is something we're consuming if we've got a little space left at the end." Find out, "We're all choosing the healthier foods first to make sure our bodies get what they need."

Through asking for her opinion while grocery shopping, you can also improve her say-so with food. She will also be pleased by preparing food in ways she likes that you know her tastes. Unfortunately, over-adjustment to finicky eating can create atypical eating behaviors that are detrimental over time.

Finicky Eating

Preparing a special meal for your daughter may be a way to show her that you love her, but she may not learn to adapt to what the family is doing when you are continually caring to her needs. And when she moves into the outside world, it won't help her. Some people might not be able to "jump through the hoops" for your daughter, for instance. Then dining at a friend's or cousin's house may be awkward for her. You can also discourage her from trying new foods if you stick to her limited range of choices constantly. It is important to have these questions.

One option is to allow your child to make their own meal if you disagree with choices about food. When she takes this course, though, it is important to clean it up later. You might say: "I've already cooked the family a full meal. If you want something special, you should make yourself a sandwich as long as you instantly clean it up. "The answer gets her to wonder if her complain was worth it.

RISK

Typically, a diagnosis of ADHD means the child is very active. However, there are risks as well as fun with those high levels of activity. Your child may enjoy the excitement, liberation from limits, and increased attention that happens when "the engine revives," but the side effect may be harmful. That's what worries you, particularly when she reacts as stifling to your attempts to protect her. Because if you don't stand in her way, there can be severe consequences, it's easy to see how power struggles can escalate when children are active.

You want your daughter to experience the world and not stay "in a bubble," but you don't want her to hurt herself either. You want her to understand that it is not worth taking those chances. But, if she feels you're too sheltering, she might completely stop listening to you. If she believes you're threatening her because you don't think she can win, she may respond defensively and dig in her heels. Therefore, walk slowly.

But even though your daughter has trouble understanding the full impact of her behavior, she doesn't have trouble understanding that you're saying no. So what keeps her from speaking to you? Unless you can solve that problem, if you want to protect her from danger, you'll need to be extremely vigilant. Sure, you should try to ban her and restrict her physically, but it may not always be necessary, sadly.

Curbing Risk

No kids want their parents to stop being involved, so when you foster vigilance, convey the message that you care for her. Make aware that your safety concerns always have to do with the world's lack of predictability, not their skill level. Let her that you love "playing it safe" before you find out more about a case. Tell her, "Are you going to help me work out how to do this carefully?"

Resolving Resistance

Despite your best efforts, it can be difficult to break down resistance to security demands, especially if siblings or peers have different limits. For example, if she sees her peers not wearing helmets, your daughter may not want to wear a bicycle helmet. She might be concerned about bullying. This may discourage her from defending herself and may raise her reluctance to respond to your sound advice. Tell her when that happens, "What do you think about teasing?" If others start to ridicule, try to help her find a way to respond.

The goal is to make your child happy and appreciate the benefits of the suggested safety measure. Unless this is done, her follow-up is questionable. In an attempt to increase "buy-in," you might ask her, "Why do you think people _____ when they do this activity [wear a helmet, wear safety glasses, etc.]?" She may be more willing to take the steps once she knows the rewards herself.

Chapter 5
Managing ADHD Behavior Away from Home

Finally, you have to leave the house, so handling ADHD behavior in the outside world is crucial. It can be dangerous to travel. For fact, if your child goes outside limits and does damage to the property of others, the result may be costly. Even, if you do not curtail the ADHD actions of your child, you risk not fulfilling your errands and upsetting strangers. When she handled herself, it would be fine, so how can you get that to happen?

PROBLEMS IN THE CAR

The new relationship you build with your child will help immensely wherever you go, but during car rides, certain unusual issues that arise. It is both aggravating and risky to drive if your kid is misbehaving. You may be in a rush sometimes, and if your daughter doesn't want to help, she will ruin anything.

Solutions

You want your daughter to put on her seat belt without being told to do so, but if she's upset with something else, she may refuse. It makes better sense to look into the source of her annoyance than to focus only on her lack of compliance. Because the backseat can be lonely, by being proactive, you can also avoid negative attention. In a conversation, you can include your daughter, pack items of interest to her, or play a game with her to make the trip less lonely and boring.

When, when driving, your child starts a commotion, you may be worried about health. You may need to find a place for the car to rest and wait for it to settle down. Yeah, maybe you're late, but it's your best option. Let your child know, "Seeing more than one child ride with you is safe to drive only if we sit in our seats and get along." When you return to the lane, though, make sure the kids stop fighting and do something else, even if it just looks out the window. If they are not distracted from the conflict, the fighting can resume quickly.

WHO SITS WHERE?

When there is constant disagreement over the seating arrangement in the car, apply the same techniques that you would use to minimize conflict within the household; help the kids figure out the sharing system they want to use. Do this before your next trip: ask the kids if they have any suggestions to fix the problem at a time when everyone is calm. Every child may have a special seating choice, but as long as the kids find out what works for them, everything is going to be fine. Make sure that their program correctly informs them, or it is unlikely to be effective, who has first preference at specific times. You don't want to keep track of whose turn it's for the seat you want.

USING THE BATHROOM

Trips are often long, and access to a toilet is not always easy. Your daughter may insist that she doesn't have to go to the bathroom until you go, but she may start complaining that she has to use the toilet shortly after she leaves. You should pause to comply easily, but try to find a solution which reduces the discomfort if the situation is routine. Let her know: "It's a long trip, and finding a bathroom will be hard. Want to use the bathroom now to make you more relaxed while we're driving?" If she says no, you might add,' We'd be happy to wait for you,' as a way to make her rethink.

Help your child get into the bathroom routine before leaving. Model what you'd like her to do and ask if she'd like to take a turn. Start the journey whether or not she is going. There may be considerable difficulty if events play poorly, but try to stay relaxed as she pays attention to her own pain. She will eventually learn that she's better off modeling your actions, and you're not going to have to say a thing about it.

PROBLEMS IN THE STORE

If you're looking for something she likes, your daughter may be very cooperative. But when she feels compelled to buy for others, her actions may be dramatically different. As is often the case, once she lacks the authority to determine what happens, the ADHD conduct of your daughter is sparked and intensified.

Solutions

If you're in good mood, your child will behave more, so you have significant influence. Talking about the favorite topics of discussion for your child can also help make unnecessary shopping less annoying. But most notably, if your child has more insight into what is going on, your child will probably comply more. If you're shopping for food, for example, you might ask her when she wants to help you decide what to get. Older kids might be happy to help you find bargains. Others may want to read the list of groceries or push the cart.

The bottom line is that when you and your child get along positively and share authority, ADHD behavior will be less frequent. Try to find the "sweet spot" where you get enough space for her to fit you easily so that you can complete the order. This is hard to achieve, but it can be achieved, and during shopping excursions, this has the biggest long-term effect on the rate of ADHD behavior.

RESOLVING PUBLIC MISBEHAVIOR

When you're out and about, things may not always go smoothly, so what do you do if your child acts up? If necessary, you should disregard or avoid the actions, but encouraging it to be loud and disruptive is not always acceptable to others. There may also be dangers when she's exuberant in public places that you don't want to play out.

Sadly, once your conduct is disrespectful or dangerous, you may have to physically stop your child or leave the store. In some situations, after a short time, it may be possible to re-enter the shop if your child settles down and you feel assured that when you return to the store, all will be optimistic.

Still, however, you might have to go back. It is crucial for your child to understand that her behaviors have a ripple effect in these circumstances. Such negative side effects can be illustrated. For starters, "Because we haven't done our shopping, we're going to have to go back later, and I'm not going to be able to make the dessert I was preparing of tonight." If the problem goes on, you might want to go one step farther. You might suggest that your daughter spend some of her own money to pay for the return trip, pointing out the positives of this option (e.g., this compensates others for having inconvenienced them, and it might mitigate their difficult feelings against her). When she offers reimbursement, everyone benefits.

Like when dealing with hygiene issues, you might also ask your child if she'd like to stay home next time and use some of her own money to pay someone to keep her company. She thus carries some of the burden of refusing to satisfy the family agenda. Offer her choices, but also let her know that it may cost her some decisions.

PEER RELATIONSHIPS

Is your child accusing other kids for achieving a sense of superiority? Trying to "buy" friends by giving away personal items, displaying low self-esteem? Should she whine of mistreatment in order to get you to run her defense? Will she always sit on the playground by herself or just play with kids out of the common circle? If so, you might want to change it. You want a fun social life for your child and feel comfortable interacting with a variety of people.

Misbehaving with Peers

Quite often, her conduct becomes excessive when a child with ADHD meets another rambunctious child. If she behaves stupidly and doesn't try to meet standards, she stops feeling inferior, and when she plays with another cap tester, there is no loss. There is power in numbers, and when she teams up with a "bad friend," your daughter gathers influence and leverage.

Solutions

You can try to keep your child away from other kids who act out. This can, however, give your child the impression of being weak and easily manipulated. Another approach is to make her realize why she is mistaken and help her handle what happens when she faces negative influences successfully. This approach sends her the impression that in her setting, she will show herself and bring about change. She will see herself as a leader with good-sense. You might say, "Your friend might be clever enough to imitate you when you're playing together."

You might also ask your daughter how she feels about getting in trouble and raise the question, "How do you want others to see you?" You can help her work out what to do when others push the envelope to find out if she's scared that if she doesn't join, others will make fun of her.

They may also question whether the cap checking is acceptable because the tricks may be misplaced ways of gaining attention or forms of weakening authority. Let your child know that addressing her problem behavior with her peers has a key advantage: taking them on family excursions makes it fun.

Doubting Acceptability

If your daughter doubts she's reasonable to others, she will find it harder to act fairly. Perhaps when she clowns around, she encourages others to grin, but the unfortunate side effect is that she gets attention for immature behavior. She briefly takes advantage of habits that will inevitably not serve her well. If that's the case, you might say, "Do you believe you're going to have to show off or do something dumb to make people like you?" Then ask, "How is this going to work for you?" When she thinks it goes poorly, inquire, "I wonder if there are other ways to attract them?" You want to maintain your child's great sense of humor, but you don't want her to be crazy or dumb. She has many qualities that other people will admire, and you want her to bring out her best foot. Her actions with ADHD that diminish significantly when she is socially comfortable and confident that she is a friendly person. Additionally, her choice of friends will probably change if she feels good about herself.

Supporting Social Development

If your child is on the younger side, she'll probably repeat a lot of habits she experiences with other adults within the family. If she is demanding and possessive with you, with her playmates, she may also be demanding and possessive. When family members manipulate or disrespect her, or others give her a hard time, she can overreact or display fear. It is important to nurture habits that fit well with non-family members for these reasons. If you want her to communicate, accept social boundaries, and conduct with her peers assertively, improve her ability to connect within the group.

It is also helpful to give your child an opportunity to interact with other kids while encouraging their social development. So she's going to increase her social skills. Encourage her effort and scheduling by saying "Let me know when you want to bring someone over so that we can make arrangements for a play date."

You might discover that your daughter wants to interact with younger children as she enjoys social power or the ability to decline and become infantile. They may also note that she is searching for older kids who are introducing her to new things and caring for her. Yet make sure that she also has contact with children of the own generation, as this provides more ways to solve issues relating to sharing and rivalry. And in her classroom, she will have to apply to this age group.

Equally important, before you speak to her about her social interactions, give your child plenty of opportunity to decide what is fair and reasonable. This will train her for the future to be socially successful. Speak to her about your thoughts if you encounter a question and help her find a good way to solve her social dilemma. You may ask, for example, "Is your friend shouting to get her to do what you want?" As with manners, she becomes more socially adept each time she seeks a workable solution. Sharing is important to the progress of society.

Problems When You Visit with Others

It can be both fun and challenging to raise a child. Being a mother can feel overwhelming when the child shows actions with ADHD. If you are helpless and isolated, your situation will deteriorate significantly. You may want to socialize badly with adult friends, but the actions of your child can make it almost impossible to handle social visits.

If your child is used to being the focus of your life, it is possible that ADHD behavior helps to maintain things that way. She always does something to bring you back when you're distracted with something else that is not all about her. Her actions in ADHD makes you stuck with her. If you're bold and taking her on a casual outing, planning to relax and enjoy your friend's company for a few minutes, she'll make sure you don't forget her. She might cause a scene. She yanks and interrupts you from your chat. She's climbing on you or making a mess and taking you away from your mate. She declines when you ask her to clean it up. You are constantly distracted by the fact that you must have to listen to her. You feel embarrassed, and a dialogue cannot be held. The question worsens when she hears you mention her poor habits. The more it reveals the actions of ADHD, the more it becomes the conversation's hot topic. And if you cut short your stay, you simply reinforce her to try to behave in the same way, and now she's got you all to herself.

Solutions

It's not only good for you to get your daughter to comply during social interactions, but it's also good for her. If she's going to be successful with teachers and others, she's going to have to learn not to be the focus of attention. She must learn to adapt and share the spotlight to what is planned. If she can't get exactly what she wants, she must learn to make the most of a circumstance. A social trip to another person's home requires all of these things, so practicing those positive habits is a great opportunity for your daughter.

WANTING TO QUIT GROUP ACTIVITIES

You will want to include your child in organized groups and extracurricular activities, as you know, it supports the physical and social growth of a child and encourages discipline. It often takes payments, contributions and a lot of effort on your part to sign up for such things. It can be painful to know that your child wants to go after jumping through all those hoops. You can find that leaving is not an option: you want her to recognize the importance of meeting commitments, build her inner strength, and learn to solve head-on issues.

To do that, you may be intimidating your daughter with retribution and demanding constant participation once she has participated in a scheduled event. After all, splitting an agreement is not good for anyone. Many count on her (and you) to keep going, and you don't want to let them down.

Your child may sometimes give in to your demands and continue to attend. But the way things are handled may not always work very well. She can "go through the motions" and hardly try; she may be humiliated by her actions. The circumstances may feel like a tragedy because you want a good experience for her, but all you get is moaning and groaning.

Solutions

You can talk to your child about the impact of her actions on her and on members of the team or group that rely on her continued involvement. You can also ask, "If you really want to quit, you'd call _____ (coach, instructor, planner, etc.) to say you're quitting?" Perhaps this will inspire her to keep up with the activity.

But a reluctance to leave may mean that the event disappoints your son. It can mean that she overreacts to a lack of success, receives negative comments from the sidelines, has personal pressure, or is scared. It may also mean she will threaten you or feel compelled to do the operation. She will be hesitant to continue to participate unless these issues are resolved.

Find a Comfortable Resolution

Your main goal is to help your child feel confident to tell you what's troubling her. You may say, "What makes it hard for you to be there?" Opening up may take some screening for her because some things are hard to admit. So don't ask her to get straight to the point.

The solution is fairly easy at times. You may ask another child, for instance, to teach your child so that she can achieve expertise without having to perform before an audience. You could encourage her to watch other kids do the event to see how it's done. Or you might ask her to mentor a less talented girl, which would improve her sense of ability.

Nevertheless, your child can continue to resist and be scared. You should split the task into less daunting phases when that happens to keep training environments as non-threatening as possible to help acclimatize her. But let her know that depression won't help her if she wants to feel better.

Stop Negligence

Your child may have signed on for an engagement on other occasions without paying enough thought to the obligation. Maybe she will quit as soon as she finds the slightest problem, and maybe she will spend your money frivolously. If that's the case, you may find that setting strict limits is important to stop the negligence. It is not fair for either of you to underwrite risky things when your kid becomes reckless. So let her know that she will have to pay a percentage of the fee before she signs up again. You can always pay her back at that time if she fulfills the duty. You want her to finish with a stake.

However, be advised: if your child is starting or stopping an activity too difficult for you, your discipline may backfire. Trying something new will raise her resistance. You want to keep her excited and daring. You don't want to think that she's stuck and awkward. If she can't get out, she might not get in, and she might learn to avoid enriching and beneficial activities. You don't want to associate "commitments" with negativity.

Chapter 6
Adjusting Your Child to School

When the behavior of your child at home and his actions at school is significantly different, ask yourself: What is the difference between these two settings? Why are there issues with one atmosphere and not the other? For example, if your son has behavioral or learning difficulties, transition to school may be very difficult of him. He may display a much more extreme ADHD attitude when he's at school compared to when he's at home. Unless, on the other hand, he is exceptionally intelligent, or if he is satisfied by the classroom arrangement, school may be far less troublesome.

Who Does the Accommodating?

Some ADHD therapies recommend programs to respond to the child's ADHD requirements. If the school does not make the recommended changes, parents are allowed to begin to pressure administrators until the modifications are made. Nonetheless, insisting that the teacher make all the changes implies a significant risk: the child may not learn to adapt to the practices of others and respond to the environment as it is.

The assumptions of parents about ADHD influence the direction they take with the issues of their child in school. They want the school to provide permanent accommodation when they believe that ADHD is a permanent biological disability. We expect that they will always rely on special services for their child. We agree that their child will always need a private assistant in the classroom, a second set of books, extra time to finish the job, desired seating, and close monitoring by all concerned.

But you don't have to take that path, as you've found throughout this book. Your child can learn to stop showing ADHD symptoms, and from the extra help he's used to, you can wean him. Although your son may potentially benefit from special services, you may concentrate on finding existing deficiencies that hold him out of school opportunities. Then you can work diligently to reduce the need for a personalized program.

When you believe your son is unable to make progress without support, try to limit how long he can need it and try to reduce it in a step-by-step system as well. For example, if he was initially able to benefit from a classroom help or a check-in person, ask yourself, what must he learn so that he no longer needs that accommodation?

Learning in Groups

He has to make a huge change from the life he is used to when your child begins school. He has to detach himself from you and meet with the demands of outsiders who want full compliance. He has to leave the safety of one-to-one contact and his comfortable home environment in order to spend most of his time mixed in with many children fighting for scarce attention.

You will spot the children with ADHD in any school classroom. Just wait for the teacher to give the "whole class" an instruction to get something done. So look at who's fidgeting, squirming, and not engaging. While the other kids follow the instructions of the teacher and listen to her speech, a child with ADHD is often unruly, not listening, and having fun with others. The whole class is interrupted by his antics. His problem-solving team approach is a significant drawback to his school success. The teacher is going to think about how the decisions and educational success will affect others.

The Difficulty of Groups

For any of the following reasons, classes may be challenging for your daughter.

- He feels disconnected
- He objects to the bullying that takes place when teams are governed by members.
- The team feels frighten, and he wants to avoid the risk of exposing its shortcomings.

The larger the group, the worse these problems can get. In order to be successful to communities, your child must learn to yield to others. He has to suspend his wishes, expand his interests, and be receptive to what is important to others. He has to collaborate, take turns, and show his skills to the public. If a lesson is given by his instructor, he must adhere to her complete control. If his family behavior is quite the reverse, all these habits can be complicated.

At home, the behavior of your child can often run counter to the family group. She may be off doing her own thing when the family is together and waiting for her to join. He can often intrude when he is not invited. He can transfer his attention to him when others have the limelight. The parents will get used to this attitude and brush it off, but his instructor will not. Your child must learn to fit in to succeed in group settings.

Solutions

It's great to spend time with your child alone to create trust. It's also important to give him plenty of opportunity to be part of a group. Bring the family as a group as often as possible to help him practice the skills in the classroom that he will need. If family members engage in activities that separate them from each other, such as watching TV in different rooms, the child struggles to know how to communicate and get along in groups. Practice is the only way the child can learn how to communicate successfully with men. Aim to have "small group" meetings where you will pose interesting topics and share your thoughts and feelings. Ask him to find out about his day and things that are important to him.

Enable him to observe and engage in a dialogue held between at least three people to develop the team manners of your child (see the exercise below). Your child can usually quickly drop out of such a discussion if he is not especially interested in the topic. Yet you can gradually encourage him to pay more attention to other subjects and take turns in a conversation. The key is to make team interaction a joy and keep him active. You will do this easily by promoting appropriate behavior: reassure him that others enjoy his company and are delighted to be a member of the group as he (a) builds on the topic in clear and meaningful ways rather than off track and (b) waits patiently until others finish before speaking.

OTHER REASONS FOR SCHOOL DIFFICULTY

In addition to difficulties functioning in teams, children living with ADHD often have trouble in school. If something hinders the success of your child in school, finding as many contributing factors as you can is important.

Learning Difficulty

About one-third of children living with ADHD have a learning disability. If your son has a specific learning difficulty, such as dyslexia (i.e., deficiency of adolescent reading), make sure to enroll him in a comprehensive curriculum. Work closely with the school and probably a professional mentor to ensure that he has the support he wants.

But it is not shocking that children with learning difficulties are more likely to show actions with ADHD; their likelihood of success is lower. They are shielded from revealing their inadequacies by their indifference and unruliness. ADHD activity, though, typically aggravates the issue. No one learns very well without experience, and training slows down as the focus shifts to the actions of the infant.

Fear of Failure

A child's worry about lack of skill can cause schoolwork ADHD actions. For example, you might find that your child neglects to write down his homework or bring home supplies, but these oversights have the powerful effect of protecting him (at least temporarily) from the struggles and disappointments he fears. Breaking the rules doesn't help him excel, so why follow the rules or play at all? The oblivion saves him from feeling like a loser.

For your child, schoolwork can sometimes be so threatening and uncomfortable that he grasps his pencil so tightly that he hurts his hand. He will second-guess his responses to such a degree that he may lose his thought process and ask you for the solution so that he will not make a mistake. He can overreact, slap, and say he's dumb. But such anger only hurts his results, even though it often allows others to ease their expectations. It can free him from the stresses he faces by speeding through a task or giving up. On the other hand, failure to finish can also benefit by delaying critical judgment for inadequate execution of the project.

Because he doesn't want to reveal his weakness, the kid may not ask questions in class. Similarly, if you check in with him and offer to help when he's doing homework, he might say impatiently, "I know, I know," so you'll leave him alone. The fact is that because it makes him feel insecure and that means that he is incompetent.

Solutions

If your son is upset by the possibility of defeat, it is very important to respond appropriately to his mistakes. If you are, he will be more accepting of his faults. Nonetheless, being overly excited over small successes may not motivate him to work hard. Let him realize that most of the time, people have to compete to achieve in meaningful ways through many hurdles.

The Benefits of Dependency

Your child's dependency on you has security and power. He will prevent venturing into the unknown by behaving in ways that trigger your protective instincts and have you take care of problems for him. Relationships are all about getting relief from difficulties for many kids with ADHD. This leaves valuable little time, however, to enjoy the company of each other in more mature ways.

As school can be the first experience of your child away from you, it can cause issues for both of you with separation, alienation, and dependence. While he may expect the same care at school that you give him at home, in a classroom of twenty-five students, that same amount of attention is impossible. He can feel even more depressed at school because he worries that he doesn't get enough adult time at home. He may want to go to school, or you may have come to get him.

The school issues of your son may be a way to make sure you don't worry about him. Problems are like a magnet, it will pull you in. Have you ever had to leave work because you received your child's call from school? He doesn't seem to know the consequences of his actions, so you come to his aid, pick up the pieces, give him a pep talk, and maybe protect him. It's hard for him to give up these privileges and they can overwhelm the whole family.

Nonetheless, it is common for parents to be worried that others are going to blame them for not doing enough, so they are doing even more. To prevent negative school effects from happening, teachers go to great lengths. After hearing his grievances and threats to give up, they end up doing much of the homework of their son. While they are fearful of the unfinished work and procrastination, their attempts to save their scores are doing very little to improve their academic ability or independence.

Social Problems

When they're in the starting lineup, everybody wants to be part of a team. But what about the benched players? If your child fails academically or socially and doesn't join in, at the far end of the bench, he becomes like a player. The excitement and interest in what is happening, like the player who never gets into the game, is likely to disappear.

He can feel uncomfortable and even quite isolated if your child doesn't get along with teachers or peers. This may boost his desire to escape and disturb, and he may have trouble going through the day of class. During adolescence, when social relations become even more important, these kinds of problems can intensify.

Noah's Story

Noah, a fourth grader, came home from school with a paper detailing many transgressions that had happened over the course of the day: he yelled in class instead of raising his hand, laughed unnecessarily, took another student's pencil (Ethan) and rushed down the hall quickly on the way to recess. Thanks to his constant overreaction, concerns are compounding. His extreme behavior made it difficult to get along with him by teachers and peers.

School staff has told Noah's family for a long time that he had "impulsive" issue. They characterized him as "impulsive," and during team meetings, they used the term "disinhibited." It seemed like Noah couldn't avoid inappropriate behavior because he had ADHD. We recommended the parents of Noah use strict training to mitigate his disability.

The parents of Noah had followed the advice in the past. Every time, though, they wanted to solve the issue differently. We tried to use a non-threatening strategy that would allow Noah to consider better ways to deal with the problems he faced. They were not interested in stopping the school from removing its recess because it was school policy. But without overwhelming him with more anger, they decided to steer him to a more constructive solution.

First of all, they called Noah to discuss what happened at class. Because Noah knew they had been generous with him over the past few months, asking them about the unfortunate events that had taken place was simple for him. Noah's parents were happy; he was speaking to them easily, and they listened to his story without questioning or evaluating what he was doing. We decided to work as a team, and Noah addressed their offer to speak frankly very well.

Instead of seeing the pencil-grabbing incident as a "disinhibited" event, his parents asked him, "Once you snatched the pencil, what happened to you and Ethan?" They knew that investigating the relationship between Noah and his classmate was important, and they learned that retaliation was the pencil grabbing. Noah had allowed Ethan to borrow his pencil, and he felt betrayed when Ethan mocked him later in the day. Noah has often been mocked by other students, and now his emotions have been hurt, and he has been angry. He knew it was wrong to snatch the pencil, so he reached out, just as many people do when they build up anger and create issues.

Noah's father then asked him if he got what he wanted from his angry responses. We understood that it was unlikely to work very well to force him to give up the revenge because he wanted to make a move. We thought Noah was more likely to try something different if he revealed that he was not working for him with his catching approach.

Once his parents felt open to change, they said empathetically, "The behavior of Ethan must have been tough on you." They then asked, "What do you want to do next time?" It was crucial that he supported the solutions because he had to live with the consequences. Our goal was to help him find solutions that could work better.

Noah agreed after debating different possibilities that it was a good idea to talk to Ethan instead of keeping the fight going. His parents asked, "What are you going to do if Ethan starts to react negatively?" Because they decided to desensitize him to what he was fearful of. Luckily, things worked well with Ethan and prompted Noah to speak to another child later in the week as a remedy.

Noah's family have figured out his racing quickly down the hall had arisen after he was humiliated by his instructor in front of the whole school. He ran into the play yard when it was time for recess because it felt good to run. Unfortunately, his hotheaded reaction had serious side effects, close to the pencil-grabbing case. This did nothing to boost his relationship with his educators or managers in universities.

Noah's parents asked him if he would like to repeat the solution with his teacher as a way to remedy this problem. They asked, "When you told your instructor what troubled you when the class is on break, would it work better for you?" While Noah believed that his instructor would listen to him, they even explored the possibility of scheduling a meeting with his teacher.

Overall, the parents of Noah had a definite goal. I wanted to help him substitute mental pacification for the physical manifestation of anger. He expected that this new way of responding would become his new habit with ample consistency and performance. They realized he wouldn't have to worry about doing it once it became a routine until he replied. He would simply react in the face of similar situations in the future in this new, socially acceptable way. This is how parents of Noah motivated him to curb his actions "out of control."

Developing the Desire to Achieve

Your son will stuff his schoolwork into his backpack as if it were trash, depending on you to sift through his documents, uncover his teachers notes, and find assignments. It's "out of sight, out of mind" for him. You end up telling him of all the stuff he's not completed yet. He tells you that he's going to do it later, but never comes later. You press him to do this, and he does all he can to squirm free.

So what can you do to help your child overcome its guilt, alienation, and social acceptability concerns? Which strategy would help him individually complete schoolwork and enjoy his school time? Forcing obedience or saving him will get him to the next class, but what will make him become a serious student who wants to accomplish himself?

Students Have a Privileged Status

Children often hate school as they feel compelled to do work without getting anything in return. For them, to be a student appears to be slaves. This way of thinking becomes so drastic that some teens choose to drop out and get a menial job rather than try to be a student.

Through teaching your child that being a student is a privileged position, you will overcome this mind-set. Let him know that others are going to be inconvenient in promoting his school success. Show him that the family can arrange schedules and subsidize any member of the family who needs to be serious about education. Let him know that knowledge gives the family (and society) unique meaning and significance. Finally, stress that while school success can lead to a lucrative job, learning has its own quality, and it can be very fun to attend school itself.

The Homework Crisis

If homework problems do not occur, ADHD specialists doubt the accuracy of an ADHD diagnosis. It's no joke. Homework puts together all the triggers for most children to cause ADHD behavior.

Homework is an incredible conflict of interest for a student. The operation requires that others provide excellent housing. When not in class, the kid has to do schoolwork. He has to come home from a work environment and do more work instead of playing. A kid rarely feels more forced. How many kids have ever asked to do homework?

It's not shocking when your kid doesn't want to spend time to read instructions or review his assignments, or when homework is on the agenda he sneaks, lies, and ignores. In reality, some kids feel so upset about homework that they choose to fail (by not doing so) rather than succumb to the perceived oppression. A refusal to do homework for other children, though, is an omission of obligation or a veiled attempt to keep loved ones interested and attentive.

A Common Response

While some parents are squeamish about allowing their child to do homework because it interferes with other things, other families often have close monitoring of homework. These parents view completion of homework as a necessary ingredient for the success of their son. Most end up badgering their child as soon as the child enters the house to begin the task. The mission turns into a nightmare he wants to escape from. Through spending hours to complete only one or two problems, he will argue, and these power struggles will monopolize the entire evening. Even the smallest homework assignment can have enormous disappointment.

Increase Your Child's Control

Your child can better handle homework if he has more input about what's going on. And figure out what plan is beneficial to him instead of deciding when, where, and how he is doing his tasks.

For example, when they work, some kids do not like segregation. Allowing your child to do his job in a common area, such as the dining room, may be helpful. Some kids prefer background music or movies. See if that works, and if it does not, revisit the problem.

Allowing your child to create their own environment can also help make homework less troubling. He must find a way to do it if he decides to get it done. You know that when he intends to finish what he is doing, he is very good at tuning out distractions. Even a loud voice may fail to unglue him when he's "on a mission."

There are plenty of options for both homework and play for your son. Removing playtime before he finishes his homework will make him much more resent the assignments. Unlike most many coercive activities, he'll lose focus if he feels he's being hassled, and the weakest noise could throw him off the job.

Develop a Routine

If you set up a daily routine for homework, your child will be more likely to complete his homework smoothly. Like a sleep response, at a given time, his body will provide a work response. When they develop a consistent way to shoot free throws, this happens with basketball players, and your child could also get a similar benefit.

Build Independence

If your child is very young, continue doing the task together on a consistent basis during a specific quiet time. Keep him company and address any things trying to overtake him. Later, by allowing him to remain in the lead while the assignment is completed, promote his self-management. Note you're making it easier; you're not doing the work for him. For starters, you could ask his opinion on what to do first when you begin your project, and check if he agrees with any recommendations you make before you continue. It reassures him that you are honoring his thoughts and finding him knowledgeable.

The more it takes care of your child, the more autonomy it gains. When he has the knack of what to do on his own, during homework time, you will switch into a counter operation. It takes you a step closer to completing your own assignments. You might say, "How about doing my house bills as you complete some of these items in your school?" At last, you're inch away, and without you, he completes his home studies. Let him know that his freedom will allow you to complete other tasks and give you more time later to play together.

Give It a Positive Twist

Through reframing it as an opportunity to practice, you will help make your child's homework more interesting and optimistic. Inform him that just as sports practice in games and events, homework is like schoolwork learning. Because during school there is typically not enough time to learn new material or show his teacher everything he can do, homework can be a chance for him to improve or sharpen his skills so he can excel in class.

Passing in Assignments

There is yet another major concern about the problem in the assignments. Most children living with ADHD also do not go through their tasks after completing the work the night before. Why is that happening?

First of all, if your child is used to making someone prompt him to put on his uniform, brush his teeth, and get his bag, why is it shocking that when he arrives at school, he does not pull out his homework and hand it in? When his instructor does not explicitly ask him to go through his work, it is "out of vision, out of mind."

In order to solve the issue, help your son to find out how he will manage to send the finished task to his teacher. Help him find the environmental trigger that will enable him to turn his job around. It's a perfect time to help him work out a "success plan" that he can implement alone.

However, there may be other reasons for the failure of your child to pass through assignments. Perhaps he didn't do a commendable job. He could escape a poor grade by not showing his work to his instructor. After all, it is more appropriate to finish the task and fail to send it in than to turn in something awful or not to do the job. Another explanation (other than thinking over his forgetfulness) is that your son is upset at you. If you're concerned about his marks, it can be a powerful weapon against you not to succeed in the test. But in the end, nothing good comes out of it, as with other despiteful reactions.

Relating to Teachers

If you have a good working relationship with his instructor, you will encourage the progress of your child at school. Yet partnerships can be compromised if you consider that his instructor is incompetent or if, conversely, his teacher thinks that you are not doing a good job of parenting. This can happen if there is no contact with you. So how do you develop a relationship with the teacher of your child?

Daily Reports

Term report cards for many years have been with us. Nevertheless, it is now normal to use daily reports to track children living with ADHD. Regular updates have been widely accepted as they have some very clear advantages. Knowing what happened during your child's school day can be very helpful. Such data helps you to deal with problems easily and avoid them before they get worse.

Problems with Daily Reports

Daily coverage can be troublesome as educators often pull parents into issues that can be easily handled throughout the day of class. As school issues leak into the evening hours, most parents are upset. Such problems instead monopolize family time, and parents are fearful of every report.

You can also be pushed into an official by the monitoring system. The child is likely to interpret school events in terms that put him in a favorable light, although his instructor is likely to point out that something completely different has happened.

Under these conditions, you might put a strain on your relationship with him if you criticize your son when you haven't seen what happened. On the other hand, if you are side by side with your child, you risk undermining the credibility of his teacher. Sadly, if you take a stand against his instructor, you might encourage future non-cooperative activities. Your child may get the message that his teacher's conduct was inappropriate, and he may wonder if listening to her makes sense at all. In particular, if your child has often felt chastised at home, he might like the fact that you are now fighting for him instead of criticizing him. At class, he will continue to create drama because he loves your encouragement. As you can see, teacher upheaval poses the same kinds of issues as in family triangles.

So be careful: there may be problems with daily reports. This is very evident when these documents rely on your child's access to resources at home. As soon as your child walks in the door, you can end up making strict decisions. You may become the judge and jury and may begin to feel like a trial in your home life. Such experiences can mess with your child's bond and make things worse.

Solutions

Through changing the meaning of the daily reports, you will stop these kinds of issues. Instead of understanding the reports as forcing you to "inspect" and "pass judgment," see them as allowing you to "share" with your child what happened during the day. They will help you enjoy his achievements and work together to solve problems. They allow you to keep up with his life and maintain an intimate and fruitful relationship with him. You don't want to put your child on the defensive with the daily reports.

You don't want him to cover or think about the news. If you see that he did something that was unacceptable, ask him, "What happened when you reacted like that?" To figure out together what he needs to do to solve the problem. If it is necessary to respond to his teacher, ask him if he wants to help write the answer. When he complains about the poor behavior of his teacher, remind him, "What contributed to this?" Help him understand the possible reasons for the actions of his instructor and help him find a way to make the best of the situation, even though his teacher did not seem to handle things very well. Even though circumstances are complicated with his teacher, it is crucial that he continue his success in class. Tell him, "How will you change your teacher?" It is helpful to say that he himself makes an improvement.

Parent-Teacher Conferences

When you speak to the educator of your son, let her know that you admire her work. Recognize that her work is very demanding and understand that she may not be able to do exactly what you want because there are a lot of kids in the classroom. Do not fault her or, conversely, take blame for the problems of your daughter.

Sharing what you learn is important: teaching the teacher what makes your child succeed and work together at home. Many of the techniques you used at home are also going to work at school. Encourage her to improve the self-reliance and co-operation of your child in the classroom just as you do in the home. Speak to her about his sensitivities in order to understand his overreactions and discuss ways of solving these issues together. For example, if your child is eager to reveal his inadequacies, she may be able to highlight his achievements and encourage him to educate another child when she discovers that he is competent with certain subjects.

Working out how your child gets along with all of his teachers, peers, and other school staff is also useful. The information that you gain will be useful in helping him solve problems that come to your attention as the year unfolds. Note if you help him establish positive relationships at school, he'll probably show more improvement in his performance and classroom conduct.

Let the teacher know about the desires of your daughter so that she can incorporate lessons and maximize her engagement. The relationship between your son and his instructor would probably improve if he understands that she is actively considering him. For example, if he's a wrestling fanatic when she offers an assignment about a professional wrestler, he might be very happy with her.

CONCLUSION

The solution offered by this book is not to monitor the child more often. It's about improving her self-care and esteem for others. You are developing a bond of mutual respect in which it is more important to receive her approval than to push her around. So stay calm, enjoy her company, and use a good tone of voice. Communicate to her, "We're together in this, so let's fix it together."

At first, your child may not like to have more responsibilities, but she'll enjoy having an input about what's going on in the end. She may also like the fact she's accomplishing, and other people respect what she has to offer. Sure, it is important that she desires, but it is also important for her to provide for others and contribute to their well-being. Your job is to help her achieve the crucial balance, as it provides her future happiness with the best opportunity.

Printed in Great Britain
by Amazon